D1607308

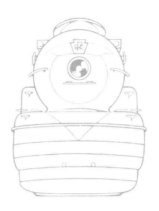

THE STEAM LINERS

STREAMLINED STEAM LOCOMOTIVES AND THE AMERICAN PASSENGER TRAIN

KEVIN J. HOLLAND

TLC
PUBLISHING INC.

TLC Publishing, Inc.
1387 Winding Creek Lane
Lynchburg, VA 24503-3776

International Standard Book Number   1-883089-70-0
Library of Congress Control Number   2001096325

Design and Production by
Kevin J. Holland
type&DESIGN
Burlington, Ontario

Produced on the MacOS™

Printed by
Walsworth Publishing Company
Marceline, Missouri 64658

Front cover —
Industrial designer Otto Kuhler injected new life into the Lehigh Valley Railroad's passenger train operations in the 1930s with successive commissions to restyle the *Asa Packer*, the *John Wilkes*, and the *Black Diamond*. In this detail of a painting by artist Michael Kotowski, one of the 4-6-2 Pacifics styled by Kuhler for the *John Wilkes* leads the train through South Plainfield, New Jersey, circa 1939. ©Michael Kotowski. Reproduced with permission.

Title page art—
Artwork depicting Pennsylvania Railroad K-4s No. 3768, adapted from a 1938 "Fleet of Modernism" brochure.

Other books by Kevin J. Holland from TLC Publishing, Inc.—

Nickel Plate Road Passenger Service—The Postwar Years
Nickel Plate Road Diesel Locomotives
Berkshires of the Nickel Plate Road
Passenger Trains of Northern New England in the Streamline Era

To a quartet of Clarkson classmates
—Doug Fear, Greg Roach, Renate Schnobel, and Dave Kerr—
for pointing the way
so long ago

to Mum and Dad, for their unfailing encouragement

and to Jenn, Graeme, and Russell, for sharing the journey

ACKNOWLEDGMENTS

Given my longstanding interest in the North American passenger train—and particularly in its development from the 1930s through the 1950s—I suppose it was only natural to be drawn in by the streamlined steam locomotives that, for a brief period, became synonymous with some of the most famous trains in the land, as well as a host of lesser lights.

My first exposure to living, breathing, streamlined steam took place at the age of 14, through windows which the architects of Clarkson Secondary School had, benevolently, positioned to overlook the Canadian National Railway's busy Toronto–Hamilton (Ontario) main line. This encounter—and the fact that it was to be the first of many—was all the more remarkable for having taken place in 1975, as the locomotive embraced an all-too-short second career in mainline excursion service for its original owner. Possessed of a conical smokebox nose, skirted running boards, rounded cab-front contours, and glossy black paint relieved by splashes of green, CNR No. 6060 was not *truly* streamlined, but hinted at the efforts made by designers to keep their locomotives looking "modern" even as their very technology was being rendered obsolete by the diesel. I was impressed, to say the least.

To Douglas J. Fear and Greg Roach goes the credit for encouraging their classmate's early glimpses through those windows, and for cultivating an appreciation and understanding of what was seen.

In another high school encounter, former Canadian Pacific Railway Royal Hudson No. 2860—visiting eastern Canada as an ambassador from its adopted British Columbia home—exhibited a somewhat sleeker form than its erstwhile rival, but it was up to the pages of *Trains*, *Passenger Train Journal*, and *Railfan* magazines to hint at the full, vanished spectrum of streamlined steam.

Relatively little has been published on this subject in book form over the years—in North America, at any rate—with Quadrant Press' pictorial review *Streamlined Steam* of 1972, edited by Eric Archer, a notable exception.

TLC Publishing's Thomas W. Dixon, Jr., was quick to accept my proposal for a book on streamlined steam, and patient as the project sometimes languished. He enthusiastically uncovered stacks of documents and images which added immeasurably to the presentation.

Ted Rose passed away before this project could be completed, but the enthusiasm and generosity of Ted and his wife Polly are manifested in the paintings reproduced in Chapter 6.

Michael F. Kotowski combined an admiration for streamlined steam with his considerable artistic skills to create the paintings gracing the front cover and Chapter 6, and I am grateful for his allowing their inclusion in the book.

Kevin P. Keefe, Associate Publisher of *Trains* magazine, generously permitted the reproduction of selected material from Kalmbach Publishing Company's David P. Morgan Library.

Harold K. Vollrath, Jay Williams, Joe Schmitz, Joe Quinn, Louis A. Marre, J. Michael Gruber, Herb Harwood, Al Paterson, and Dave Shaw all permitted the use of images from their collections, as did the New York Central System Historical Society, the Chesapeake & Ohio Historical Society, and the Denver Public Library.

Donald Bain, John B. Corns, Geoff Doughty, Larry Goolsby, Eugene L. Huddleston, Doyle McCormack, Ken Miller, Mike Schafer, Robert J. Wayner, and Joe Welsh each provided information and encouragement.

To all, my sincere thanks.

"There is no excellent beauty,
that hath not some strangeness in the proportion."
Francis Bacon, *Essays*, 1625.

2 PREFACE

4 WINDS OF CHANGE
STREAMLINING EMERGES

16 UNCHARTED TERRITORY
1934 – 1936

52 MOMENTUM
1937 – 1939

102 AGAINST THE ODDS
1940 – 1950

136 NORTHERN PARALLELS
CANADIANS AND KIN

148 THE SPECTRUM
STEAMLINERS IN COLOR

156 BIBLIOGRAPHY

PREFACE

Webster's defines a fad as "a practice or interest followed for a time with exaggerated zeal."

Should the streamlining of steam locomotives be defined—or worse, dismissed—as a fad? Hardly.

The evolution of railroad motive power and popular culture collided in the 1930s, in both Europe and North America. Streamlined steam was but one result.

Students of railroad history, for the most part, have not been kind to streamlined steam—on a good day, granting grudging admiration to successes like the Milwaukee Road's *Hiawathas*, while, at worst, dismissing lesser efforts as little more than sideshow oddities ... the "what" at the expense of the "why."

Streamlined steam locomotives were, and remain, both products *and* victims of their time—harbingers of the future and, at the same time, a pruned branch on steam's evolutionary tree.

The emergence of industrial streamlining during the early 1930s coincided, in large measure, with an awakening desire of North American railroads to replace steam locomotives with more efficient,

more economical, and—particularly where passenger trains were involved—more attractive forms of motive power.

Streamlining became the next logical step in the evolution of passenger train motive power—nascent diesel-electric technology decreed that many of these locomotives happened to be steam.

The history of North American railroading records that the steam locomotive, as a dominant force deemed worthy of continued development, was in decline as America's railroads embraced lightweight, streamlined passenger trains and the sleek, colorful diesel-electric locomotives built to pull them.

Times were changing, mechanically as well as esthetically, with the streamlined steam locomotive perhaps best regarded not as a faddish aberration, but as an inevitable step in the "natural" evolution of the locomotive form, whether it be electric, steam, or diesel. Some of the earliest American streamlined steam locomotives—including the first, New York Central's *Commodore Vanderbilt*—were noted for their broad, sloping "shovel" noses, an aerodynamic styling trait shared

The consummate "steamliner"—the 1938 edition of the *20th Century Limited* departs Englewood, Illinois, for New York City behind J-3a Hudson No. 5454 on August 6, 1944. RICHARD J. COOK

with such internal-combustion contemporaries as the Budd-built Burlington Route *Zephyrs* and Boston & Maine-Maine Central *Flying Yankee,* and the Gulf, Mobile & Northern's *Rebel.* The pioneering EA-model passenger locomotive built by Electro-Motive for the Baltimore & Ohio—along with the smaller TA's built for the Rock Island— took the shovel nose to the next evolutionary step, creating the "covered wagon" cab and nose architecture that would rule American railroading for close to two decades. Different packages, indeed, the *Commodore* and the cab-unit, but sharing a common wrapping.

Styled by some of the leading industrial designers of the day—and their emulators—the "steamliners" were caught in an unfortunate limbo, often derided by steam stalwarts as an affront to their purist tastes, yet just as readily dismissed by disciples of the dawning diesel age as tawdry dowagers out for one last self-conscious fling.

THIS BOOK ATTEMPTS TO distill and present the place of the steam locomotive in the evolution of North American streamlined design from the 1930s through the early 1950s. It explores the industrial design trends impacting—and impacted by—the locomotives and the trains they pulled, and, as such, deliberately avoids delving too far into mechanical minutiae. Design and engineering specifications and selected diagrams are, however, presented as points of comparative reference.

One of the earliest decisions regarding this book's structure—how best to segregate material—was also one of the toughest, and came back to haunt more than once. Streamlining, and the streamlining of steam in particular, was an evolutionary process, and a chronological presentation therefore made the most sense. This dictated the establishment of somewhat arbitrary time periods for each main chapter. Adherence to this "flow" created a few disruptions that may, at first glance, seem odd—separating the Milwaukee Road's early and later *Hiawatha* incarnations into three chapters, for instance, and similar placement of the distinct "chapters" in the Pennsylvania and Baltimore & Ohio railroads' streamlined steam stories.

Emerging from such a chronological presentation, though, are some intriguing patterns involving the increasing confidence of the designers, and the often inter-related traits of their designs.

Now, the big question ... What *is* a "steamliner"? The term itself appears to have been coined in the late 1930s and was used by several American railroads to publicize new streamlined steam locomotives *and* steam-powered streamlined trains. Therein lies the problem in crafting a nice, clean definition. Not all streamlined steam locomotives were assigned to streamlined trains ... nor were all steam-powered streamlined trains pulled by streamlined locomotives. The most readily defined "steamliners" were the stem-to-stern package deals—the *Mercury,* the *Crusader,* the 1938 *20th Century Limited,* the 1941 *Empire State Express,* the *Cincinnatian,* the *City of Memphis*—all of which were streamliners conceived, built, and originally operated with streamlined steam as an integral component. All of these, and more, are represented in the following pages, as are trains like the *International Limited, Merchants Limited,* and *Black Diamond,* rendered "steamliners" by virtue of their shrouded locomotives alone. The final qualifiers are more subjective ... those streamliners—Pennsy's prewar "Fleet of Modernism" chief among them—that rated unstreamlined steam power for part of their careers. Some of them are here—and a few oddities, too.

1 WINDS OF CHANGE

A taste of things to come. One of two Pacifics streamlined by designer Henry Dreyfuss for New York Central's *Mercury* paces an unclad, but younger, Hudson along the latter's namesake river south of Harmon, N.Y., on May 15, 1936. The occasion—publicity runs for motion picture and still cameras. NYC PHOTO; NYCSHS COLLECTION

The period between the First and Second World Wars, remembered for its political and economic upheavals in Europe and America, left an equally tumultuous legacy in the fields of architecture and design.

Europe was a crucible of emerging design influences in the early 1920s, with the German *Bauhaus*, Austria's *Wiener Werkstätte*, and the British Arts and Crafts movements among those leading the way from the classical adornments of previous decades and centuries towards a cleaner, "modern" esthetic.

The pavilions and manufacturers' displays of the *Exposition des Arts Décoratifs et Industriels*, held in Paris in 1925, showcased the vanguard of European design and architecture, and became a catalyst of style on both sides of the Atlantic. Fittingly, the exposition's name became synonymous, in abbreviated form, with what would become the prevailing design movement of the late 1920s and 1930s—Art Deco.

Although the convenors of the 1925 Paris exposition extended an official invitation to the United States, American designers and manufacturers were absent from the ranks of exhibitors. Reflecting on the exposition, designer Paul Frankl wrote in 1928 that "the only reason why America was not represented at the Exhibition ... was because we found that we had no decorative art. Not only was there a sad lack of achievement that could be exhibited but we discovered that there was not even a serious movement in this direction and that the general public was quite unconscious of the fact that modern art had been extended into the field of business and industry."[1]

While they may not have had the wherewithal to become exhibitors, American designers, manufacturers, and government representatives *did* attend the exposition as observers, and upon their return planted the seeds of a lucrative and far-ranging design revolution—not, however, without its critics. Herbert Hoover, then U.S. Secretary of Commerce, dispatched a three-person commission to review the exposition and, in conjunction with several dozen officially sanctioned delegates, prepare an official follow-up report on their observations.

The critics spoke, among them delegate Richardson Wright, who regarded the Parisian displays as "the most serious and sustained exhibition of bad taste the world has ever seen."[2]

The more entrepreneurial delegates, along with Stateside observers, encouraged manufacturers and market forces to be heard above the critics' ire, however, and by 1927 Art Deco furnishings, jewelry, and graphic elements had been introduced to American consumers by retailers such as Saks Fifth Avenue, Macy's, and Lord & Taylor. The public appetite—at least at the most affluent levels—had been whetted in 1926, when nine American museums, foremost among them New York's Metropolitan Museum of Art, hosted a traveling exhibition of selected pieces from the 1925 Paris display. Macy's, still priming the pump, held an "International Exposition of Art in Industry" in 1928. The following year, the Metropolitan Museum once again showcased Art Deco trends in an interior design exhibition titled "The Architect and the Industrial Arts."

The nationalist pride, progress, and prosperity experienced by broad segments of American society in the decade following the First World War marked the United States' emergence as a world power, both political and economic. Europe lay eviscerated, the British Empire was beginning to shrink, and the future, it seemed, belonged to America. The imagery of the Art Deco movement—clean-lined, bereft of classical adornment, and utterly modernistic—reflected American society's embrace of a bold, progressive future. Art Deco, in turn, would be embraced and hybridized by America and, within a decade of the Paris exposition, would become a pervasive force in American popular culture.

COLLECTIVE VISION

An influx of European architects, artists, and designers, immigrating to the United States after the First World War to further their collective vision, helped spread the gospel of Art Deco across America. Among them were several who would leave particularly important legacies in the fields of architecture and transportation.

Eliel Saarinen, a Finnish architect and staunch modernist, arrived in the U.S. in 1922 and subsequently established the Cranbrook Academy of Art, a Detroit-area haven for similarly inclined emigrés. Saarinen's son Eero would leave his mark on the American transportation landscape with striking terminals at New York's Idlewild (JFK) and Washington's Dulles airports, and was also responsible for the Gateway Arch at St. Louis.

Raymond Loewy, French by birth, had moved to the U.S. in 1919 and, after several years as a fashion illustrator in New York, became widely known for his 1929 restyling of the Gestetner office duplicator and the 1935 Sears Coldspot refrigerator. Beginning in the mid-1930s, Loewy undertook wide-ranging design projects for the Pennsylvania Railroad, foremost among them his cosmetic restyling of the GG-1 electric locomotive. With an eventual client list as eclectic as his lifestyle, Loewy and his firm would inculcate themselves to the American corporate and cultural landscape with commissions

for the likes of Chrysler, Sears-Roebuck, Studebaker, Nabisco, AT&T, Greyhound, Douglas Aircraft, Standard Oil, United Airlines, TWA, Coca Cola, and the U.S. government. Loewy's work for the latter included the elegant restyling of John F. Kennedy's presidential Boeing 707 (known, then as now, by the call sign "Air Force One" when the Chief Executive is aboard) and interior design for NASA's Skylab. His firm's railroad portfolio extended beyond the Pennsy to include Northern Pacific, Delaware & Hudson, Norfolk & Western, Missouri Pacific, Southern Pacific, Canadian National, Fairbanks-Morse, and the Baldwin Locomotive Works, among others.

Otto Kuhler, a painter and graphic artist of considerable talent, came to the United States from his native Germany with a fascination for America's industrial infrastructure. Fittingly, he arrived in 1923 aboard the liner *Pittsburgh*. Seeing the streamlining of established forms as a means of modernizing the public's perception of the railroads in the face of increasing air and highway competition, Kuhler published conceptual drawings that gained widespread attention. Among the earliest of these were his 1927 proposals to streamline New York Central's recently delivered Class J-1 4-6-4 Hudsons. In his subsequent career as an industrial designer, Kuhler amassed a portfolio of distinctive styling commissions for the American Locomotive Company (Alco) and railroads as disparate as the Milwaukee Road, Baltimore & Ohio, Lehigh Valley,

Although Raymond Loewy did not style the original Pennsylvania Railroad GG-1—shown here at its August 1934 debut—he earned a lasting reputation, and many future PRR commissions, by smoothing its riveted carbody and redesigning its striping and lettering. The prototype GG-1 was a watershed in the adoption of streamlined sheathing for American locomotives—steam, diesel, *and* electric. GENERAL ELECTRIC PHOTO; AUTHOR'S COLLECTION

Otto Kuhler's conceptual streamlined locomotive designs received wide exposure through the 1930s. The "Wings on Wheels" Alco ad appeared in March 1934, while the 1938 Standard Steel Works ad employed Kuhler renderings of the mid-1930s. AUTHOR'S COLLECTION

Southern, New York, Ontario & Western, and Gulf, Mobile & Northern.

Winold Reiss, a German muralist and interior designer, would be noted for his contribution of stunning mosaics to the rotunda and concourse of Cincinnati Union Terminal, opened in 1933 and itself one of the most enduring icons of Art Deco architecture in America.

Paul Cret left his native France prior to the First World War, becoming a Professor of Design at the University of Pennsylvania in Philadelphia before entering private practice as an architect in 1907. Following a wartime return to Europe, he won civic commissions across the United States, culminating in 19 buildings designed for the University of Texas while he served as that institution's consulting architect from 1930 to 1945. In the early 1930s, Cret also lent his design talents to the first generation of lightweight, streamlined passenger trainsets then under development by Philadelphia's Budd Company. The signature fluted stainless steel exterior of Budd's passenger cars was Cret's handiwork. He is also remembered for his involvement in Cincinnati Union Terminal as consultant to project architects Fellheimer & Wagner, with credit for CUT's remarkable appearance going mainly to Cret. John F. Harbeson, a former student and, later, colleague of Cret's, and a partner in the Philadelphia architectural firm of Harbeson, Hough, Livingston & Larson (the successor to Cret's firm upon his death in 1945, known today as H2L2), would maintain Cret's link with the Budd Company by consulting on the interior decor of some of Budd's most famous postwar streamliners.

Foremost among contemporary American-born industrial designers was Norman Bel Geddes (the father of actress Barbara Bel Geddes). Following early work as a New York and Hollywood set designer, Bel Geddes' first industrial design commissions were a series of concept automobiles for the Graham-Paige company, the first appearing in 1927. Furniture and appliance designs for Simmons and other manufacturers coalesced into the publication of visionary—some said propagandist—proposals for homes and cities of the future, which in turn led to Bel Geddes' central role in designing pavilions and exhibits for the 1939–40 New York World's Fair. Bel Geddes' work in the transportation arena was equally progressive. His 1929 "Air Liner No. 4" proposed a 20-engine, flying-wing behemoth—unfulfilled, but it foretold the demise of the ocean liner's supremacy and led to a 1934 commission to design the interiors of a series of Pan Am's *Clipper* flying boats. His 1931 proposal for a steam-powered, streamlined train was years ahead of its time. Although unrealized in its conceptual form, many elements of Bel Geddes' luxurious design would find their way into streamliners of the later 1930s and 1940s.

Henry Dreyfuss was best known in a railroad context for his work on New York Central's *Mercury* of 1936 and the 1938 edition of the *20th Century Limited*. Henry Dreyfuss Associates, as the firm he founded in 1929 is still known, amassed a portfolio mirroring rival Loewy's in its diversity. Designs produced by Dreyfuss' office included such icons as the Bell Model 302 and 500 desktop telephones,

Walter Dorwin Teague styled these streamlined passenger cars built at Pullman-Standard's Osgood Bradley Works in Worcester, Mass. Along with the New Haven, the Boston & Maine was an early operator of this 1935 design. Their reproduction in model form earned them the nickname "American Flyer" cars, after the line of toy trains marketed by the A. C. Gilbert Company.
BOB'S PHOTOS COLLECTION

the circular Honeywell thermostat, the Hoover Model 62 vacuum cleaner, a range of John Deere tractors, the teardrop-bodied Hughes 500 helicopter, and enduring corporate images for American Airlines, John Deere, and Pratt & Whitney.

Walter Dorwin Teague styled what were among the earliest streamlined passenger cars to enter service, the so-called "American Flyer" cars built by Pullman-Standard's Osgood Bradley Works and operated originally by the New York, New Haven & Hartford Railroad. Similar cars followed for companies in New England, the South, and the Southwest. Like Loewy and Dreyfuss, Teague's office undertook widespread commissions for competing modes of transport, most notably as designers of cabin interiors for the Boeing 707 and its derivatives.

NEW MATERIALS, NEW METHODS

The widespread adoption of Bakelite™ (introduced in 1909) and subsequent early plastics like Durez and Catalin, with their low cost and ease of manufacture, along with the increasing affordability and availability of materials like aluminum and stainless steel, meant that millions more Americans were exposed to "the future" as manifested by the Art Deco movement. The novelty and escapism provided by the new materials' shapes, colors, and applications were particularly appealing as the Great Depression usurped the optimism and prosperity of the 1920s. "Dimestore Deco," as the mass-produced cornucopia was dubbed, found its way into every corner of the country.

As the 1930s dawned, architectural tastes underwent a shift to the new style, driven in large measure by the public works erected by Franklin Roosevelt's Works Progress Administration (WPA) and Public Works Administration (PWA). The linear Egyptian and Mayan influences—both structural and decorative—pioneered by Frank Lloyd Wright, Bruce Goff, and others—were clearly in evidence, and would become closely linked with American Art Deco architecture and design.

Egyptian imagery was still fresh in the public conscious after Howard Carter's 1922 discovery of Tutankhamen's tomb. Public awareness of pre-Columbian cultures in the Americas had been broadened in 1928 by Franz Boa with the

publication of his *Primitive Arts.* Mayan, Aztec, and Incan influences became favorites of ceramic and textile designers, and the bold geometry and color palettes were readily adopted by practitioners of early Art Deco architecture. Skyscrapers of the period—William Van Alen's Chrysler Building of 1930 the crown jewel among them—were liberally adorned with interpretations of such "High Deco" imagery, before a more austere and streamlined "Moderne" form of Art Deco was embraced by American architects on projects such as New York's Rockefeller Center, begun in 1931.

Motion pictures provided a welcome form of escapism during the depression, and, through the films themselves and many of the theaters in which they were shown, exposed innumerable Americans to their first glimpses of Art Deco and streamlined design. Films such as *Broadway* (1929), *The Easiest Way* (1931), and *Big Business Girl* (1931) were among the earliest examples of such public cultivation to emerge from Hollywood, several years after Marcel L'Herbier's *L'Inhumaine* (1924) and Fritz Lang's *Metropolis* (1926) debuted with similar, if somewhat more sinister, visual overtones in Europe.

Prophetically, the Department of Commerce's *Report of the Commission on the 1925 Paris Exposition*, released in 1926, had observed that "... the United States represents the greatest consuming public in the world—one with the highest standards of living and one that is constantly availing itself of novelties in its household and business life. Furthermore, in no other nation are the facilities for transmitting new ideas to the mass of the people so highly developed, and in no other nation is the response so immediate when interest is aroused."[3]

When the Bauhaus closed in 1933 in the face of German political upheaval, many of its adherents moved to the United States. With Walter Gropius, Ludwig Mies van der Rohe, Josef Albers, and their colleagues came a fresh infusion of European design insight—in this case, the gospel of functionalism and its applicability to depression-era American architecture and industry.

The concept of streamlining—in a railroad context, at any rate—had existed as far back as 1865, with the patenting by Reverend Samuel Calthrop of designs for

40 YEARS AGO
Everything Streamlined
But the Bell Rope . . .

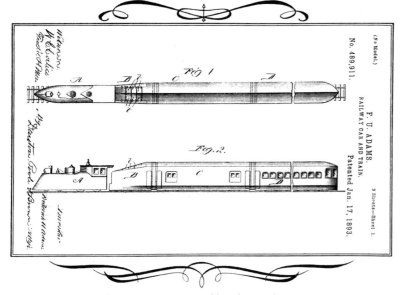

IT is mighty interesting right now to note patent No. 489911 granted to F. U. Adams on January 17, 1893 covering a Railway Car and Train.

Quoting from the patent paper, "This invention has reference to the construction of railway trains with the primary object of diminishing atmospheric resistance to their movement and with the ultimate object of making a higher speed of such trains attainable with a given expenditure of motive power."

Note the smooth canopy construction attained by the continuous outer surface, closing up the gaps between the cars. Even the apron covering the trucks extends right to the end giving the effect of one long car. Note the vacuum drag — also the front end construction of the locomotive which fairly splits the wind — also the sand box and cab. In fact, everything streamlined except the bell rope.

It seems odd that Mr. Adams, over 40 years ago, came so close to the designs that are attracting so much attention today.

AMERICAN LOCOMOTIVE COMPANY
30 CHURCH STREET · NEW YORK · N.Y.

Frederick Adams' streamlined train proposal of 1893, like Samuel Calthrop's 25 years before, sought the benefits of what came to be known as aerodynamics.
AUTHOR'S COLLECTION

an "air resisting train." Those were the days of the *Monitor* and *Merrimac*, and design elements of these benchmarks of naval modernism were evident in the teardrop styling of Calthrop's articulated steam locomotive and coach. Calthrop characterized his train, tapered both fore and aft, as a ship moving not through water, but through air, and devised its streamlining accordingly. Jules Verne and other contemporary writers popularized enlightened but whimsical proposals for "windsplitter" trains and flying machines. U.S. patent No. 489,911, issued to Frederick Adams on January 17, 1893, described a steam-powered passenger train employing methods of construction "with the primary object of diminishing atmospheric resistance to [its] movement and with the ultimate object of making a

higher speed ... attainable with a given expenditure of motive power." In 1900, the B&O conducted tests on equipment based on Adams' patents but did not pursue further developments. Eight years later, William McKeen unveiled a knife-prowed gas-electric motor car designed to minimize wind resistance. Over 100 were sold prior to the First World War, but widespread streamlining on America's railroads was still two decades away.

Followers of the Italian Futurist movement theorized applications for streamlining in the first decade of the 20th century, but went no further. While aviation's first three decades were characterized by winged machines of decidedly unstreamlined appearance, their lighter-than-air dirigible counterparts were shining, if incendiary, examples of the favorite Bauhaus maxim of form following function.

Coincident with the practical debut of streamlining—made possible by the artistic talent and industrial diversity then available in America—was the emergence and acceptance of the field of industrial design, spearheaded by Norman Bel Geddes, Walter Dorwin Teague, Henry Dreyfuss, Otto Kuhler, and Raymond Loewy. Beginning in the mid-1920s, when Teague and Bel Geddes each opened design offices, and gaining momentum through the turn of the decade when both Loewy and Dreyfuss began courting corporate clients, industrial America was being awakened to the importance of packaging and marketing its output in order to spur consumer demand. *Fortune* magazine summed up the far-reaching transformation of the manufacturing and distribution process in 1934 when it said, "Furniture and textiles had long sold on their design. Now it was the turn of washing machines, furnaces, switchboards, and locomotives."[4]

While critics like the Metropolitan Museum of Art's John McAndrew were quick to question the wisdom of streamlining immobile objects such as radios and kitchen appliances, and as quick to deride the end results, the public—through such pervasive vehicles as the Sears-Roebuck catalog—spoke with their sparse dollars to inseparably link this Moderne form of Art Deco with 1930s America.

Norman Bel Geddes had stated in 1932, with characteristic vision, that, "In the perspective of 50 years hence, the historian will detect in the decade of 1930–40 a period of tremendous significance. ... he will ponder that in the midst of a world-wide melancholy owing to an economic depression, a new age dawned with invigorating conceptions and the horizon lifted."[5]

Indeed. The ensuing marriage of industry and design—although blessed with its share of curious offspring—forever changed the way America and the world regarded the act of moving from "A" to "B."

CLEAN OF LINE

When Donald Douglas unveiled his company's DC-1 airliner prototype in June 1933—in response to Boeing's then-abuilding Model 247 and a 1932 design specification from Jack Frye of Transcontinental & Western Air (TWA)—and promptly followed this first Douglas Commercial design with the production DC-2 and DC-3, he led commercial aviation firmly into the streamline era.

Form followed function. Stalwarts of the first generation of fledgling airliners—ungainly collections of fabric surfaces, wood, and wire like the aptly named Curtiss Condor, and even metal-skinned pioneers like the Ford Tri-Motor—were rendered immediately obsolete in terms of speed, range, durability, capacity, and—perhaps most significantly—public perception. The application of aerodynamic design and lightweight alloys—pursued by aircraft designers following the pioneering work of Jack Northrop—also caught the attention of those charged

with developing a new generation of railroad passenger train.

Cross-pollination was the order of the day. The earliest purpose-built American streamlined trains—with their minimal protruding appliances, quasi-tubular car-bodies-cum-fuselages, sealed windows, and teardrop-contoured rear ends—borrowed heavily from contemporary developments in aviation. Lacking the sleek wedge profile of the new Budd-built *Zephyrs*, the power cars of Union Pacific's contemporary *Streamliners* (M-10000 and M-10001), Illinois Central's *Green Diamond* of 1936, and even the first non-articulated locomotives assigned to the Overland Route's *City of Los Angeles* and *City of San Francisco*, on the other hand, had their bulbous prows adorned with enough Detroit-inspired chrome grillwork and trim to do Flash Gordon proud.

Railroad passenger cars fabricated from aluminum or stainless steel were inherently lighter than the heavyweight steel arks then populating railroad and Pullman Company rosters and, all else being equal, required less fuel and horse-power to haul from point to point. The Pullman Car & Manufacturing Corporation calculated in 1934, albeit somewhat muddily, that 1280 horsepower would be required to move a representative three-car conventional (non-articulated) train at a sustained speed of 100 miles per hour, while a lightweight, three-car, articulated trainset could achieve the same speed using only 488 horsepower. Pullman advertisements in support of this message showed something of an apples-to-oranges

The Douglas DC-3 was an enlarged version of the DC–1 and DC-2. Collectively, the design of these aircraft revolutionized aviation, and aspects of their architecture could be seen in streamlined railroad equipment by the mid-1930s. *Sky Chief Acoma* was one of several DC-3 types operated by the Atchison, Topeka & Santa Fe's short-lived postwar air-freight subsidiary, Santa Fe Skyway. AUTHOR'S COLLECTION

Union Pacific acquired its first lightweight, articulated train from Pullman-Standard in 1934. The second, in 1935, did indeed mark a trend, in company with the Burlington Route's *Zephyrs*. The streamlined passenger train had arrived. AUTHOR'S COLLECTION

comparison, illustrating trains of obviously different capacities, and stressed aerodynamics over the more fundamental reduction of car weights, but the point was nonetheless made.

As a means of reducing fuel consumption, lightweight construction was of much greater value than streamlined styling, yet the two became synonymous. Designers of railroad equipment needed not lose sleep over wind resistance (drag), and attempts to reduce it, to the degree that the subject preoccupied their aeronautical counterparts. One inherent benefit of streamlining, however, was the improvement of air flow over the locomotive and thus a reduction in the tendency of smoke to obscure the crew's vision while the engine was "drifting." This had, in fact, been the prime objective of wind-tunnel testing undertaken by Canadian National in 1931, early in the development of Canada's first streamlined steam locomotive, CNR's Class U-4a of 1936. Improved aerodynamics was a secondary benefit, and was largely negated in all but head-on winds. The pressure exerted by oblique or broadside winds created considerable added friction where the "downwind" flanges contacted the rails, whether the locomotive and cars were streamlined or not.

Streamlining, then, as applied to railroad equipment, was for all practical purposes a public relations endeavor intended to forestall declining ridership.

Otto Kuhler underscored this in a November 15, 1935, presentation to the New York Railroad Club, stating, "Every competitor in passenger transportation, and many of those transporting goods alone, have taken advantage of sales appeal as expressed by streamlining." Going on to summarize recent developments among airlines and bus operators, Kuhler observed, "Streamstyling, on railroads, therefore, comes to a large extent in the field of the sales department, the passenger traffic manager and, with limitations, the freight traffic manager."

The number of persons riding American passenger trains had been in decline every year since 1921, to the degree that ridership had dropped by 58%—over 600 million *fewer* passengers—just 12 years later in depression-wracked 1933. Figures quoted in *Railway Age* for the five-year period 1934-1938[6] indicated that the decline had been stayed, with modest increases of approximately 34 million additional passengers in each of the five years. Credit was given in large measure to the crop of new lightweight streamliners' having used their speed and novelty to lure daytime passengers out of competing buses.

In the span of less then two years, the streamlined carapaces applied to Electro-Motive passenger diesels went from grilled to bulbous to sublime. Power unit No. M-10004 of the original *City of San Francisco* (above, at right) contrasted its 1936 "Buck Rogers' visage with more-refined styling of adjacent E2. The evolution of Electro-Motive cab design is clearly evident. The first of what the builder termed its "Streamliner" series was EA No. 51, built for B&O in 1937. Sibling No. 54 shows off the EA's remarkably smooth nose contours. Streamlining and motive power were undergoing a parallel metamorphosis. ELECTRO-MOTIVE PHOTOS; AUTHOR'S COLLECTION

The new trainsets made headlines, and many barnstormed to offline cities and towns throughout the East and South prior to entering revenue service for their owners, affording untold thousands of potential passengers a peek at the future.

Industrial designers like Kuhler, Teague, Dreyfuss, and Loewy repackaged their clients' locomotives and passenger cars and cloaked them in an unprecedented palette of colorful liveries, all to elicit the attention—and the patronage—of a travel-ing public increasingly tempted by equally modern airliners and highway vehicles.

"The man in the street," said Kuhler in his November 1935 remarks, "does not know anything about high-pressure boilers, feedwater heaters, roller bearings, etc., and above all, he does not care. He only sees the locomotive as a steam locomotive and, if locomotive Model 1936 looks like Model 1916, he refuses to be impressed. Even the best and biggest advertising will fail to convince him."

Kuhler knew only too well that this rationale for streamlining also applied to diesels and electrics. "Just as with the streamlined steam locomotive," he said, "variety on the front end of Diesel-electric trains is possible. Shape and color may be used for identification." His first streamlining effort had been a rather restrained mid-1930s "clean-up" of Alco's high-hood diesel switcher carbody, followed by a thorough and sleek exterior streamlining of the Gulf, Mobile & Northern's *Rebel*, a lightweight train built by American Car & Foundry and powered by Alco in 1935.

This pursuit of stylishness by the railroads and their designers was even more apparent inside the new crop of "streamliners." To borrow from Hemingway, they were a "movable feast" of visual and culinary stimulation, in many cases rivaling the exclusive clubs and restaurants familiar to their well-heeled passengers. Trains like the Santa Fe's star-studded *Super Chief*, along with the streamlined incarnations of New York Central's *20th Century Limited* and the Pennsy's *Broadway Limited* immediately became synonymous with the ultimate in style and luxury.

A FAIR TO REMEMBER

With the United States in the throes of a deepening depression, streamlining was seen in some quarters as a metaphor for economic recovery, with President Roosevelt even urged in 1934 to make the movement the foundation of America's financial resurgence.

Streamlined Art Deco imagery figured prominently in the Century of Progress Exposition, held in Chicago in 1933-1934 to promote "advancement through technology," but it was the New York World's Fair of 1939-1940 that is remembered as the apogee of Moderne Deco in all of its futuristic splendor. These two fairs would be seen in later years as bookends of the American Moderne movement's most fertile period, during which expositions also were held at San Diego (1935), Dallas (1936), Cleveland (1936), and San Francisco's Treasure Island (1939).

Symbolized by J. Andre Fouilhoux's and Wallace Harrison's starkly suggestive "Trylon and Perisphere"—respectively, a 699-foot obelisk of triangular cross-section connected to a 180-foot-diameter steel sphere—the New York World's Fair carpeted Flushing Meadows, Queens, with a 1216-acre collection of government and corporate pavilions showcasing a Utopian future all too soon pre-empted by war.

Walter Dorwin Teague served as chairman of the New York Fair's organizing committee, and Bel Geddes, Loewy, and Dreyfuss were among those with whom he shared responsibilities for pavilion and exhibit design.

Glimpses of transportation in the "world of tomorrow" were everywhere— some, predictably, more theoretical than practical—with Bel Geddes' General

World's Fairs bracketed the decade and the country, and whetted the public's appetite for better times that seemed always just around the corner. AUTHOR'S COLLECTION

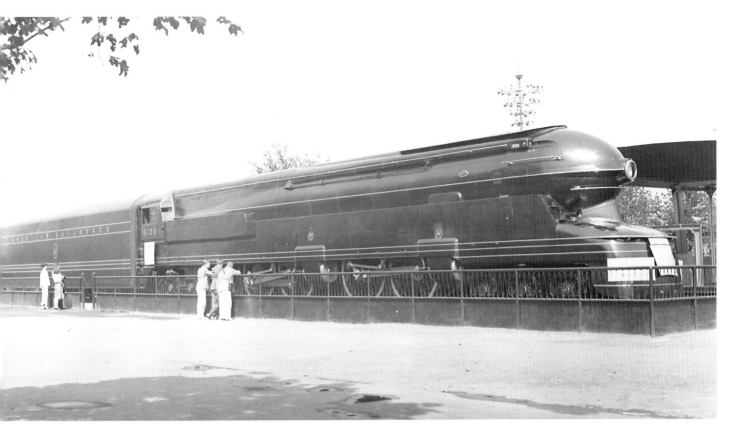

Motors "Futurama" and Loewy's transatlantic rocket service tempered by in-the-flesh displays of the latest in streamlined conformity from America's automakers and railroads.

Steam locomotives had yet to be vanquished from the main lines of North America, and the 45 million fairgoers could compare and contrast Electro-Motive's latest E3 passenger diesel—with its gracefully slanted nose and smooth contours evoking the early Budd *Zephyrs*—and, "alive" on a nearby treadmill, the svelte duplex-drive 6-4-4-6 styled by Loewy for the Pennsylvania Railroad (but temporarily lettered "AMERICAN RAILROADS" in a nod to the Fair's magnanimity).

FOOTNOTES TO THE FUTURE

While streamlining and railroading had embarked on a journey that would continue, in fits and starts, into the 21st century, the steam locomotive's place in the streamlined spotlight would last barely a decade (almost twice as long in Canada), dampened by the exigencies of war and finally extinguished by the virulent eventuality of dieselization.

Streamlined steam, then, was both a product *and* a victim of the times. Evolution of popular design tastes and the

emergence of the profession of industrial design gave rise to the streamlined locomotive form when steam was—for a few years, at least— still king, just as surely as the almost-simultaneous evolution of locomotive propulsion ensured that the vast majority of streamlined locomotives would be diesel-electrics.

"American Railroads" No. 6100, styled by Raymond Loewy, on its treadmill at the 1939 New York World's Fair. In 1939 and again in 1940, the London, Midland & Scottish Railway gave American railroaders a look at one of Britain's streamlined speedsters. ABOVE, JAY WILLIAMS COLLECTION; BELOW, AUTHOR'S COLLECTION

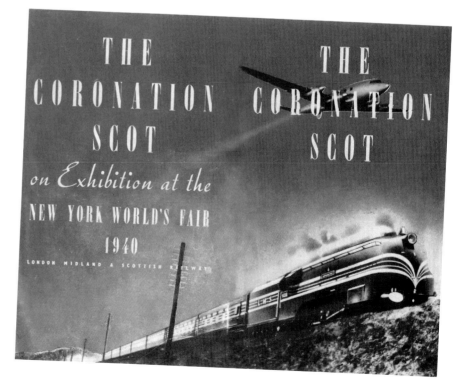

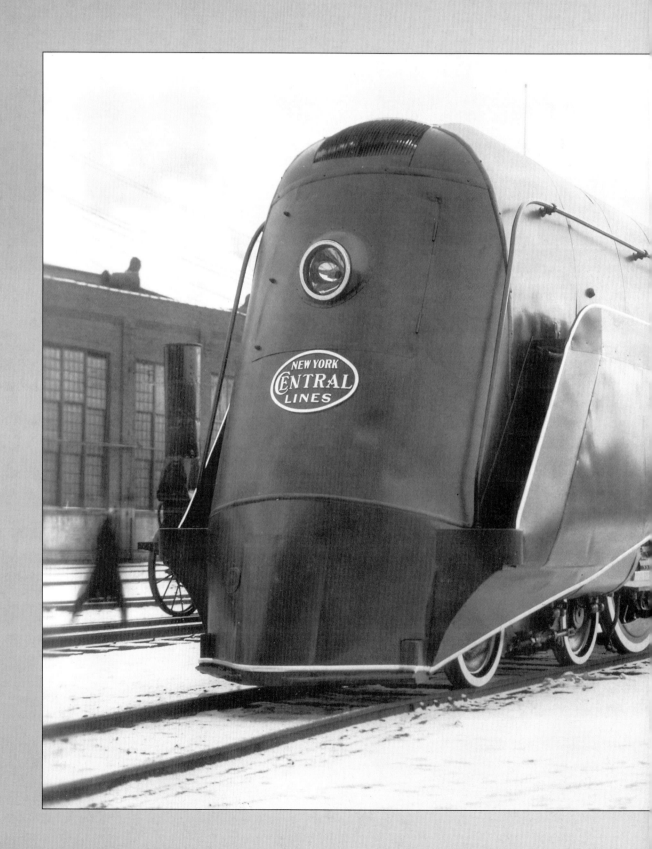

New York Central's *Commodore Vanderbilt* was America's first streamlined steam locomotive. Named for the railroad's founder, shrouded J-1e Hudson No. 5344 was unveiled at West Albany, N.Y., on December 14, 1934. NYC PHOTO; TLC PUBLISHING COLLECTION

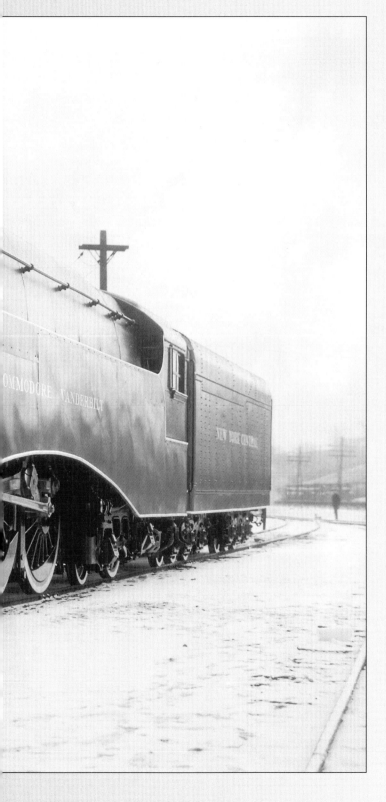

So seductive was the allure of streamlining to American railroads in the early 1930s that, but for a late change of plan dictated by economics, the first streamlined steam locomotive in North America would have been used not in high-profile passenger service, but at the head of fast freight trains.

Beginning in 1934, the American Locomotive Company (Alco) devoted much of its advertising space in *Railway Age* and other trade publications to promote its willingness to design and build streamlined steam locomotives. The New York, Chicago & St. Louis Railroad (the "Nickel Plate Road"), with the benefit of access to its own considerable design and engineering resources in the form of the Advisory Mechanical Committee, had placed an order with Alco for the construction of ten 2-8-4 Berkshire

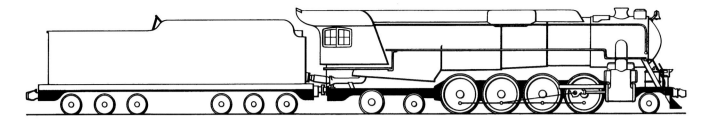

Had plans to apply conical noses and skyline casings not been dropped to cut costs, Nickel Plate Road 2-8-4 Berkshires Nos. 700-709 would, in all probability, have been first off the streamlined steam blocks in 1934. COPYRIGHT KALMBACH PUBLISHING COMPANY, REPRODUCED WITH PERMISSION

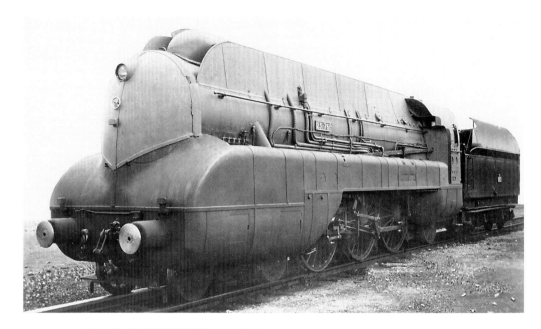

European railroads were in the vanguard of streamlined steam design. These three French designs date to the early 1930s and exhibit efforts to reduce both aerodynamic drag and smoke-related cab visibility problems. ALL, AUTHOR'S COLLECTION

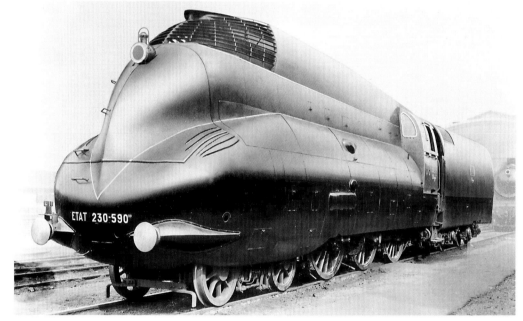

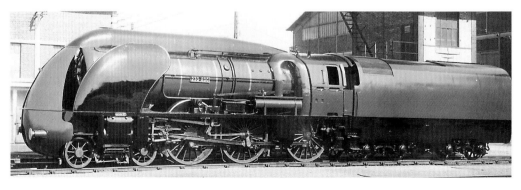

locomotives. Intended to revitalize the Nickel Plate's ability to compete for time-sensitive freight with the largely parallel New York Central, an eventual 80 AMC-design Berkshires would accomplish this and more as they made "Nickel Plate" synonymous with "High Speed Service." None, however, would bear the torpedo streamlining proposed for the first order.

TRAINS OF THOUGHT

Alco and the AMC were not alone in testing the waters of streamlined steam in 1934. Canadian National, employing wind tunnel tests on models at Canada's National Research Council, had been developing streamlined shrouding for application to a group of 4-8-4 Northerns beginning in 1931, although the locomotives would not be built until 1936 (see Chapter 5).

Recognizing as Alco did that the dawning generation of lightweight, streamlined internal-combustion trainsets posed a threat to the entrenched steam builders' livelihood, Lima Locomotive Works' vice-president Will Woodard proposed a high-speed, semi-streamlined 4-4-4 in the summer of 1934. Woodard, an accomplished locomotive designer regarded as the father of steam's "Super Power" era, described "a straightforward combination of established basic features with important innovations in detail development." He favored a 26-inch piston stroke, poppet valves, and four-coupled 84-inch drivers—the first pair attached to the main rods—as an arrangement combining speed with "the smoothest possible running characteristics." Woodard observed on the subject of speed and four-coupled drivers that, "we are apt to forget that this was one of the great virtues of the old eight-wheeler." By his calculation, an output of 2,200 horsepower would convey a 250-ton train at a sustained 90 MPH.

A progressive pragmatist, Woodard envisioned "a general design prepared for securing as much advantage of streamlining as is consistent with accessibility of parts for inspection and maintenance." He limited his proposed shrouding to a skyline casing, which he described as a "hood extending from the stack to the cab and covering dome, sand box, safety valves and turret. This hood at the rear

end merges into the front of the cab structure." Drawing upon European influences, his 4-4-4 was equipped with "elephant ear" smoke lifters that blended into the skyline casing.

Developments in Europe had shown that the French, Germans, and British were in the vanguard of those striving to extract new levels of speed and aerodynamics from the steam locomotive.

In Great Britain, the Chief Mechanical Engineer of the London & North Eastern Railway (LNER), Sir Nigel Gresley, designed the wedge-nosed A4 Pacifics of 1935, which gained immediate fame in service on the lightweight *Silver Jubilee* between London and Newcastle. This 268-mile run was made at an average speed of over 67 MPH.

The London, Midland & Scottish Railway's Chief Mechanical Engineer, Sir William A. Stanier, oversaw the design of that company's Coronation-class Pacific.

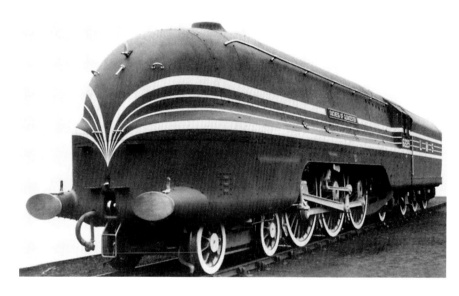

Of 38 eventual examples, 24 built between 1937 and 1943 were fully shrouded. One of these, No. 6229 *Duchess of Hamilton*, swapped name and number with No. 6220 *Coronation* for a 1939 visit to the New York World's Fair. The streamlined Pacific was transported across the Atlantic in February 1939 with an eight-car display train aboard the *SS Belpamela*. War had broken out in Europe by the time the Fair concluded its 1939 season, so the British locomotive and train remained in New York as exiles—much like the ill-fated French Line ship *Normandie*, berthed across town. The British train was exhibited at the Fair again in 1940, after which the cars were

Duchess of Gloucester was one of Sir William Stanier's 24 fully streamlined Coronation-class Pacifics. BRITISH RAILWAYS PHOTO

19

requisitioned by the U.S. military for use as an officer's club. The streamlined LMS Pacific, however, was needed back home and returned to Britain, regaining it original name and number, in February 1942.

As more designers entered the North American streamliner fray, the elevation of style for style's sake—Woodard's pragmatism notwithstanding—became an inevitability. Alternately praised by traffic departments and cursed by operating staff, full shrouding offered a sculptured canvas for increasingly colorful liveries, but at the same time added weight and obscured or hindered access to running gear and components requiring ongoing attention. The same zeal to conceal was evident in streamlined passenger car design, where underbody components and even trucks were hidden behind hinged skirts.

Otto Kuhler was particularly blunt in his 1935 appraisal of emerging trends in steam locomotive streamlining. Addressing the New York Railroad Club that November, Kuhler observed, "Streamline freak locomotives have been built lately the world over. Most of them are badly conceived in their outline and their shrouding and covering; in most of them the inherent beauty and the 'personality' of the steam locomotive is lost."

Given his ties to Alco at the time, Kuhler worded his criticism of full shrouding carefully, and with a qualifier: "... the ultimate aerodynamic streamline form is not justified under today's and tomorrow's operting conditions in this country. ... In no case, if correctly conceived and correctly streamlined, does the shrouding have to be ugly. That it can be made beautiful has never been shown more spectacularly than in the performance of the new streamstyled colorful train *Hiawatha*... ."

Kuhler then confirmed where his own styling preferences lay. "It is entirely wrong to assume that all future engines have to look like the streamline locomotive on the *Hiawatha*."

Some did, including a later Milwaukee Road group styled by Kuhler—apparently at the customer's behest. Virtually all of his ensuing streamlined steam creations, however, were notable—and acclaimed—for the manner in which, in Kuhler's words, "the characteristic features of the steam locomotive have been retained in the streamlining."

THE LORD AND LADY BALTIMORE

Theorizing had already moved toward application in early May 1934, with the announcement that the Baltimore & Ohio had secured a $900,000 Public Works Administration (PWA) loan to permit the construction of two lightweight eight-car trains.

The second such loan to be awarded (the first having gone to the New Haven Railroad to finance its bidirectional, articulated *Comet*), the government money was intended to fund what amounted to a demonstration project. One B&O consist would be constructed of high-tensile, corrosion-resistant Cor-Ten steel, and the other of aluminum. One was intended to be steam-powered, the other hauled by a diesel-electric locomotive.

Both trains would operate between Washington, DC, and metropolitan New York City over the joint B&O-Reading-Jersey Central "Royal Blue Line," affording comparisons between the two aforementioned motive power options and the Pennsylvania Railroad's newly electrified service. That was the B&O's original plan, at any rate.

The "Royal Blue Line" was launched in 1890 in the face of Pennsylvania Railroad intransigence—the B&O and PRR had wrangled over division of the route's traffic for years, with the Pennsy never shy about throwing around its weight. By 1890 the B&O had had enough, and partnered with the Reading and Jersey Central to reach to Gotham beyond its own recently established railhead at Philadelphia.

The first consist delivered from American Car & Foundry's St. Charles (Mo.) works was assigned to operate not on the "Royal Blue Line" but over the B&O's Chicago & Alton subsidiary (the Alton Route) on a 5.5-hour schedule between St. Louis and Chicago.

Christened the *Abraham Lincoln*, the eight blue and gold Cor-Ten steel cars entered revenue service on July 2, 1935, after completing a far-ranging promotional tour through the Midwest and East. The train was displayed at 43 cities in eight states between May 15 and the first week of June. During a pre-inaugural test run between St. Louis and Chicago, the train achieved an average speed of 62.2 MPH and sustained 80 MPH or better for 124 miles of the 284-mile route.

Baltimore & Ohio's *Royal Blue* was inaugurated as a lightweight, streamlined train between Washington, DC, and greater New York City on June 24, 1935. Motive power alternated between 4-6-4 No. 2, named *Lord Baltimore*—shown leading the train across the stone viaduct at Relay, Md.—and diesel-electric boxcab No. 50, a pioneering Electro-Motive unit. B&O PHOTO

The streamlined equipment replaced a slower northbound train between St. Louis and Chicago, and provided an entirely new southbound service. Alton passengers had the option of identical-duration schedules between these end-points on no fewer than three competing railroads, but the *Abraham Lincoln* was an immediate moneymaker for the B&O. In September 1935, for example, early in its career, the train earned just over

$77,000 in gross revenue against direct operating costs of just under $21,000.

The second consist delivered by AC&F was actually the first to enter revenue service. These eight aluminum-bodied, steel-framed cars, otherwise twins of their shopmates from interior appointments to exterior paint, became the Washington, DC–Jersey City (N.J.) *Royal Blue* on June 24, 1935, exactly one week before the *Abraham Lincoln's* revenue

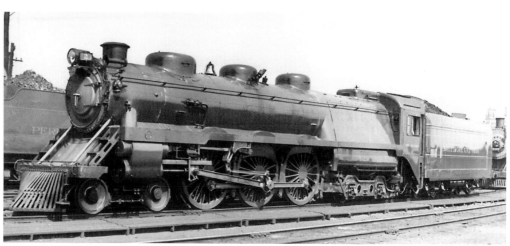

service debut. Covering a four-hour schedule on the 223.6-mile route, the *Royal Blue* emulated the earning power of its Midwestern twin—its earnings in August 1935 were approximately 50% higher than those of the train it replaced.

Despite—or perhaps because of—its modernity, the *Royal Blue's* aluminum consist did not deliver the smoothest of rides. Just two years after their debut—upon the introduction by B&O of a re-equipped, heavier *Royal Blue* (described in Chapter 3)—the aluminum AC&F cars were sent west to augment the St. Louis–Chicago service. The former *Royal Blue* trainset entered service as the Alton's *Abraham Lincoln* on July 26, 1937. At that time, the Cor-Ten steel consist was renamed the *Ann Rutledge.*

Slightly more than a year before, on April 27, 1936, the *Abraham Lincoln* had become a diesel-powered train with the transfer of B&O No. 50. This pioneeing diesel-electric was purchased from Electro-Motive with a portion of the PWA funds in 1935. In its original guise as a boxcab, No. 50 shared motive power duties on the *Royal Blue.* It proved to be underpowered at speed, however, on portion of the route. By the time of its 1936 transfer to the Alton, the 1800-HP No. 50 had been given the slight esthetic benefit of a shovel nose.

Primary power for the new B&O trains at their introduction was a pair of steam locomotives rebuilt and modernized by the railroad at its venerable Mount Clare (Baltimore) shops. Streamstyled rather than streamlined, the two exhibited decidedly Anglicized styling traits—the handiwork of B&O motive power arbiter Colonel George H. Emerson, and a legacy of the 1927 visit by the British locomotive

King George V to B&O's centennial festivities. The most immediately apparent of these was the method of securing the B&O engines' smokebox doors. Emerson abandoned the multiple circumferential bolts of American practice in favor of the yoke-and-clamp British system, in which two external bolt handles (resembling the hands of a clock) tighten first a pair of interior yokes and then an external locknut to firmly clamp the door shut. Also very British were the running board "fenders" above the *Lord Baltimore's* drivers.

TOP: B&O No. 2 and the *Abraham Lincoln* trainset pause at Washington Union Station in early 1935 during a pre-inaugural display tour. BRUCE FALES; TLC PUBLISHING COLLECTION

ABOVE: The display train passes through Youngstown, Ohio. G.A. DOERIGHT; TLC PUBLISHING COLLECTION

BELOW: *Lord Baltimore* cut a dashing, if antiquated, profile with its smoothly jacketed boiler. B&O PHOTO; AUTHOR'S COLLECTION

No. 1, the newly christened Class J-1 *Lady Baltimore*, was a sinewy 4-4-4. No. 2, the *Lord Baltimore*, was a beefier 4-6-4 Hudson, Class V-2. Common ground between the two coal-fired locomotives included 84-inch drivers, Emerson water-tube fireboxes, 61.75 square foot grate areas, and 350 PSI steam pressure. *Lady Baltimore* emerged from Mount Clare in the fall of 1934, with her consort completed the following January.

The *Lord Baltimore* exerted a tractive effort of 34,000 pounds vs. the rather slippery 4-4-4's 28,000 pounds—both, however, were equipped with boosters capable of adding 7,000 pounds starting tractive effort. *Lady Baltimore's* tender held 14

A front-end view of *Lord Baltimore*, on display at Washington Union Station, shows the two handles of the British yoke-and-clamp method of securing the smokebox door. For a brief period in May 1936 the engine's slatted pilot was sheeted over. BRUCE FALES; TLC PUBLISHING COLLECTION

Lord Baltimore is in full stride with the *Royal Blue* west of Pennington, N.J., in April 1937, shortly before locomotive and cars were sent west for St. Louis–Chicago service on the Alton Route. Note the adoption of a slatted door for the retractable front coupler. HAROLD K. VOLLRATH COLLECTION

tons of coal and 8,000 gallons of water, to *Lord Baltimore's* 16 tons and 10,000 gallons. Both tenders matched the trailing cars' height and profile and were equipped with water scoops, permitting on-the-fly refilling from track pans on the "Royal Blue Line," the only stretch of the B&O so equipped.

Vestibule cabs and a full-width diaphragm on the rear of the tenders helped each steam locomotive blend with the cars, and some utilitarian sheet metal and retractable couplers attempted to reduce front-end clutter, but streamlining in the emerging sense was not pursued.

In combination, though, these two trains were the first steam-powered lightweight consists to be delivered to—but not the first to be placed in service by—a U.S. railroad.

All three new B&O locomotives were painted royal blue to match their trains, with gold-leaf lettering. Although of lightweight construction and low-profile, streamlined design, the AC&F rolling stock was conventional in the sense that is was non-articulated, with each car an independent vehicle riding on a pair of four-wheel trucks.

They were—and were promoted as—the first "lightweight cars of the full standard size," even though they were some 16 inches lower than the heavyweight cars they supplanted. Although they had the same exterior width as older cars, the AC&F architecture and lightweight components actually yielded three more inches of useful width inside the cars. Full-width diaphragms, folding steps, and flush windows contributed to the new trains' aerodynamics.

Side-sill riveting provided a handy means of telling one trainset from the other—the steel cars had a double row of heavy rivets running the length of their side sill, just above the underframe skirts. On the aluminum cars, three rows of rivets could be seen.

As built, each train contained 283 revenue seats, divided among three coaches, two parlors, and an observation-parlor. A baggage-mail car and lunch counter-diner rounded out the original eight-car consists. The Cor-Ten steel trainset weighed in at 780,800 pounds, approximately 40 percent lighter than conventional heavyweight equipment which, comparably outfitted, would have tipped

the scales at 1.3 million pounds. The aluminum trainset was even lighter, at 699,540 pounds.

Duryea cushioned underframes were employed on each car, as were Ohio Brass (O-B) tight-lock couplers with integral steam, air, and electrical connections. Cushioned underframes would find much favor with freight car designers in later years, but their application on passenger equipment was unusual and likely contributed to the uneven ride characteristics of the steam-powered *Royal Blue* consist. Although the two steam locomotives' tenders were equipped with the same integral O-B couplers, regular steam, air, and signal lines were provided for compatibility with other equipment.

As modern as they were on the outside, the new trains' interiors—with the exception of the dining/lunch counter car—reflected an earlier era. Chairs, tables,

draperies, and light fixtures were decidedly Colonial in appearance, appropriate, perhaps, given the B&O's rich history and the conservatism of President Daniel Willard, but at odds with the message of modernity being sent by the new streamliners' comparatively sleek exteriors.

"Comparatively," because of the profusion of rivets and roof vents that cluttered the cars' otherwise clean lines and marked a not-quite-complete transition to the "new order." This was more than offset, however, by the observation cars, which adopted the tapered rear-end configuration pioneered by Pullman's experimental *George M. Pullman* of 1933.

The transfer of recently built Electro-Motive EA diesel No. 52 from parent B&O to the Alton (as its No. 100A), along with shovel-nosed No. 50 already there, bumped the *Lord* and *Lady Baltimore* from the streamliner spotlight.

THE COMMODORE VANDERBILT

The honors for America's first fully streamlined steam locomotive went to the New York Central, with the December 14, 1934, debut at West Albany, New York, of restyled three-year-old J-1e 4-6-4 Hudson No. 5344, the *Commodore Vanderbilt*.

The *Commodore's* wedge-nosed shroud, designed by Norman Zapf and Carl Kantola with the benefit of wind-tunnel tests conducted at Cleveland's Case School of Applied Science, shared unmistakable traits with the Budd *Zephyrs*.

NYC management sought data on the operational benefits of such a streamlined locomotive, and road tests—with a string of heavyweight cars—were conducted to calculate the increase in drawbar pull brought about by the shrouding's reduced drag. The wind-tunnel studies indicated that the shrouding, as applied, would reduce head-on wind resistance by as much as 30% at train speeds of between 60 and 80 miles per hour, with a corresponding 2.5% to 12% increase in locomotive drawbar pull.

New York Central's streamlined *Commodore Vanderbilt* was promoted in conjunction with the railroad's New York–Chicago flagship, the *20th Century Limited.* AUTHOR'S COLLECTION

The *Commodore Vanderbilt* prepares to lead the *Century* out of Chicago's La Salle Street Station in June 1937. A more permanent Art Deco landmark, the Board of Trade Building, looms in the distance. NYC PHOTO; NYCSHS COLLECTION

NYC publicity gushed, "This pioneer creation, named the *Commodore Vanderbilt*, marks an epochal advance in the design of powerful, high-speed steam locomotives whose possibilities in safe, reliable and fast operation have by no means been exhausted."

Derided as little more than an "inverted bathtub" by purists, No. 5344's sheet-metal shroud, attached to a contoured framework of carlines, was painted a dark gunmetal gray and accented with aluminum striping and lettering. Progressive, yet conservative, the locomotive's considerable publicity value was keenly exploited by a railroad in the throes of reinventing its "Great Steel Fleet" of heavyweight passenger trains. Brochures and advertisements routinely featured the *Commodore Vanderbilt's* unmistakable form speeding blurred consists of nondescript—but not quite conventional— cars into the future.

Pragmatism dictated that the locomotive's running gear be kept accessible for en-route lubrication and maintenance. This was achieved by arching the sheet metal above the engine's wheels and providing upward-hinging panels for access to less-vital components.

The *Commodore's* tender was also streamlined to a remarkable degree. The top of the coal bunker was enclosed with a series of latched doors, hinged at both sides and meeting along the centerline, that performed the dual functions of maintaining a smooth air flow and keeping down coal dust. A recess at the rear top of the tender shroud gave access to the cistern hatch.

Roller bearings, initially applied to engine truck, driver, and tender axles, were refitted to the locomotive's main rods, side rods, and crossheads prior to the conclusion of non-revenue testing, as were Scullin disc drivers.

Following considerable technical assessment, publicity, and display, the streamlined *Commodore Vanderbilt* made its revenue-service debut leading the heavyweight *20th Century Limited* on February 19, 1935. It was a regular on this flagship train between Toledo and Chicago until 1937 and—at least for those in the know—a portent of things to come.

After migrating to less-celebrated NYC trains, No. 5344 became one of only two American streamlined steam locomotives to be *re*streamlined when it received a completely new shroud for Chicago–Detroit *Mercury* service in July 1939 (see Chapter 3).

FLEET OF FOOT

Alco's stated willingness to build streamlined steam paid off with a 1934 order for a pair of 4-4-2 Atlantic-type locomotives designed to pull the Milwaukee Road's two new six-car *Hiawatha* streamliners between Chicago and the Twin Cities. The *Hiawathas* were America's first non-articulated streamliners, and the first streamliners to be hauled by steam. Alco outlined the "five very sound reasons" that steam propulsion was chosen for the

Hiawathas: "First; we can secure most easily and economically with steam all the speed that any railroad will dare use for many years to come. Second; the required horsepower will be secured at one-quarter of the initial investment of any other choice .... Third; the full horse-power output of the steam unit is available at or near the cruising speed. This is practically essential in high-speed work. Fourth; with the surplus power available under steam the railroad has a flexibility or margin of power which makes it possible to attach more cars when the demand arises. Fifth; a power unit capable of being maintained and operated with present railway facilities and organization."

Alco may have been willing to explore internal-combustion options, but these subtle—and very public—swipes at the lightweight, articulated trains then emerging betrayed the builder's fundamental sentiments. "For high-speed passenger service over long runs," declared the company, "with due consideration for the comfort and safety of the traveler and economy for the operating company, the American Locomotive Company offers the streamlined steam locomotive as best suited to the traditional principles of good railroading."

Their arrival preceded by a series of "teaser" trade publication advertisements placed by Alco, America's first purpose-built streamlined steam locomotives literally burst upon the scene when appropriately numbered Class A "Milwaukee-type" No. 1 tore through a bunting curtain as it rolled out of the builder's Schenectady, N.Y., works on the afternoon of April 30, 1935. The occasion was deemed of sufficient importance that, not only did Alco President William C. Dickerman ceremoniously "deliver" the locomotive to Milwaukee Road President H. A. Scandrett, but New York Governor Herbert H. Lehman was among the invited guests in attendance.

The locomotive that emerged evoked the shovel-nosed bathtub shroud of NYC's *Commodore Vanderbilt*—the Hudson freshly bestowed with streamlined form just a few miles away at West Albany—but with a striking orange, maroon, gray, brown, and black *Hiawatha* livery, and styling accents that lent an aura of pent-up motion. The A's contours were rather more rounded than the *Commodore's*,

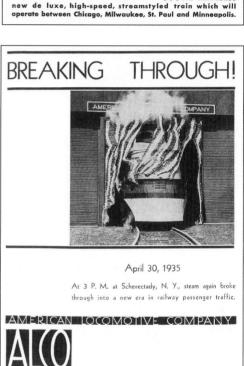

Otto Kuhler's hand was evident in much of Alco's advertising during the early and mid-1930s. The "Milwaukee Type" designation never really caught on for these locomotives—Atlantics they remained, or just simply "A's".
AUTHOR'S COLLECTION

and the Milwaukee engines' running gear was partially hidden behind skirting that matched the height of the trailing cars' side sills. Stainless steel wings, adorned with each locomotive's road number, were splayed across the gray nose beneath the headlight. Bold maroon striping was employed to good effect, camouflaging the running boards and carrying the livery's strong horizontal lines back across the tender and into the trailing orange-sided consist.

This "speedlining" (as the visual packaging was termed by Alco) was largely the work of Otto Kuhler but was a marked departure from the torpedo-like conceptual designs favored in his contemporary speculative renderings and most of his subsequent steam locomotive streamlining commissions. Pre-delivery renderings and miniature mockups of these first *Hiawatha* locomotives exhibited most elements of the as-delivered shrouding, but reveal that exposed running gear was considered. An early rendering of a *Hiawatha* trainset shows the brightly painted cars led by a recognizable, streamlined 4-4-2 in gleaming *black*—old habits died hard as America's railroads embraced the streamlined age. Speed, streamlining, and color, the industry quickly learned, could be a powerful and profitable triumvirate.

Class A Atlantics Nos. 1 and 2 headed west from Schenectady in early May 1935, and were promptly dispatched on a series of test runs and public displays.

Depression-weary Midwesterners flocked trackside to catch a glimpse of the much-touted speedsters. Observers and

Class A's Nos. 1 and 2 were delivered by Alco, amid much fanfare, in May 1935. No. 2 gleamed at Minneapolis on August 23, 1935. JAY WILLIAMS COLLECTION

No. 3 followed in May 1936, and No. 4 completed the class in April 1937. All four received large stylized "Hiawatha" figures on their tender flanks. No. 3 was photographed at the Milwaukee shops on May 24, 1937. MILWAUKEE ROAD PHOTO; AUTHOR'S COLLECTION

No fewer than 11 men give Class A No. 2 a rubdown at Chicago in April 1937, demonstrating how well the running board was camouflaged by the wide bands of color. Note the location of the bell, and its slotted door, above the retractable coupler's compartment.
J. MICHAEL GRUBER COLLECTION

railroaders alike wanted to see how the Milwaukee Road hoped to best the already established Chicago–Twin Cities competition of the Burlington Route's diesel-powered, stainless steel *Twin Zephyrs* and the Chicago & North Western's steam-powered but as-yet-unstreamlined *"400s."* (The C&NW trains derived their unusual name from the Chicago–Twin Cities route's 400-mile length, and their 400-minute end-to-end timing set the benchmark for rail competition between these two endpoints.)

To Class A No. 2 went the honors of pulling the first full *Hiawatha* consist—on a test run on May 15, 1935—and attaining a speed of 111.5 MPH in the bargain. That velocity, as duly reported in *Railway Age*, was maintained for the better part of three miles in the course of the 141-mile Milwaukee–New Lisbon (Wis.) run, and the smoothness of ride encountered

aboard both engine and cars validated Milwaukee Road management's aspirations for their new *Hiawathas*.

Additional test runs were made, one of which saw No. 2 lead an 11-car heavyweight *Pioneer Limited* consist with ease. On a May 24 Chicago–Milwaukee round-trip special for 259 members of the Traffic Club of Chicago, speeds between 106 and 108 MPH were maintained for 20 miles between Deerfield and Mayfair, Illinois.

Public displays gave potential passengers—138,310 of them—an up-close look at the new trains in Chicago, Milwaukee, the Twin Cities, Red Wing (Minn.), Winona (Wis.), and La Crosse (Wis.), and tantalized off-route residents in Janesville, Madison, Beloit—all in Wisconsin—and Rockford, Illinois. The railroad employed advertisements in 70 newspapers nationwide to spread word of the new trains. Full-page, color newspaper ads appeared in the key on-line endpoints of Chicago, Minneapolis, and St. Paul—only the second time that a railroad had used color in that medium, and never before so extravagantly.

All of the anticipation culminated in the May 29, 1935, inauguration of *Hiawatha* service in the form of Milwaukee Road trains 100 and 101 over the 410 miles between Chicago Union Station and the Twin Cities. Festivities in Chicago, broadcast over radio station WLS, included the christening of the train by Jeannie Dixon, daughter of Milwaukee Road General Passenger Agent W. B. Dixon. Chicago Mayor E. J. Kelly and Milwaukee Road President H. A. Scandrett offered appropriate remarks, after which listeners heard the first westbound *Hiawatha's* departure. Its eastbound counterpart was given a similar send-off in Minneapolis.

The *Hiawathas'* initial schedule allowed 390 minutes for the trip, at an average speed (including five intermediate stops) of 63 MPH. Eastbound and westbound trains both departed at 1:00 pm, and arrived at their respective endpoints at 7:30 pm. Engineers entrusted with the svelte Atlantics had ample opportunity to hit the route's official 90 MPH speed limit, and even brushed the century mark—with management's tacit approval—as warranted. Created for speed and speed alone, the Class A's were designed to achieve 120 MPH.

The Class A's exerted their 30,700 pounds of tractive effort through 84-inch Boxpok drivers. Among their other vital statistics: 19x28-inch cylinders; 300 PSI boiler pressure; 144,300 pounds weight on drivers out of a total 290,000 pound engine weight; and tender capacity for 4,000 gallons of fuel oil and 13,000 gallons of water.

As with all streamlined steam, beneath the cosmetic shroud was a conventionally recognizable locomotive, with firebox, boiler, smokebox, stack, cylinders, and other appurtenances located just where convention dictated they should be. As was the case with the *Commodore Vanderbilt*, the Atlantics' shrouding was, for the most part, fabricated from sheet metal and supported on a strip-metal contour frame. Given that the Milwaukee A's were designed from the outset to be streamlined, portions of the shroud were more integral than was possible with an "aftermarket" streamlining. The exhaust

stack casting, for example, incorporated lugs to which 16-gauge steel shroud panels were attached, and the lower front-end shrouding was of sufficiently rugged fabrication to serve as the locomotive's pilot. Skirting extended approximately 33 inches below the running boards. The upper front-end shrouding opened clamshell-style for access to the smokebox, and small latched doors were provided elsewhere for access to other hidden components subject to regular inspection. Horizontal grillwork flanking the headlight admitted a smoke-lifting airstream that was exhausted immediately behind the stack while underway. A slotted compartment above the retractable coupler held the bell, while a Leslie Tyfon horn—operable by either air or steam—was integrated above the headlight.

The adoption of a vestibule-style cab, with doors and a diaphragm filling the normally open gangway area, contributed to the *Hiawathas'* clean lines and was no doubt appreciated by crews during upper Midwest winters.

Class A No. 4 was assigned not to a *Hiawatha*, but to lead the Milwaukee Road's *Olympian* west from Chicago Union Station on June 1, 1938. This view shows the smoke-lifting air intakes to good advantage. The circular opening above the headlight was an air horn. J. MICHAEL GRUBER COLLECTION

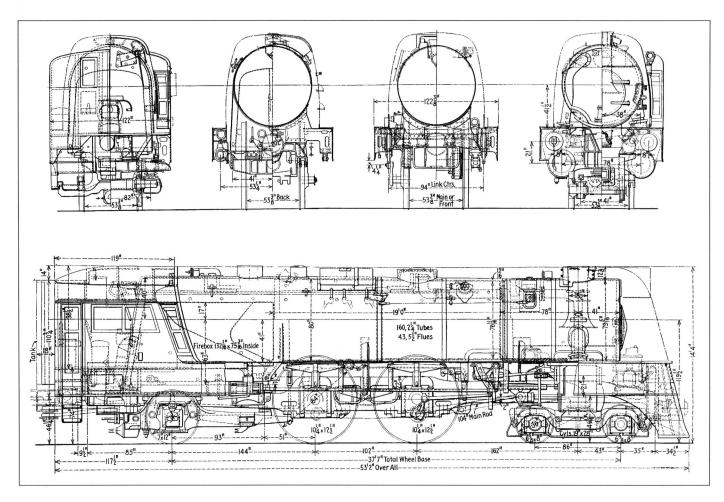

These cross-section and elevation drawings reveal how the Milwaukee Road Class A Atlantics' shrouding was fitted over the locomotives. RAILWAY AGE

Roller bearings on locomotive and car journals and the choice of oil as fuel contributed to the *Hiawathas'* ability to maintain their demanding schedule. Roller bearings became a staple of the streamlined era, shortening running gear inspection and maintenance times and reducing the potential delays and danger of overheated friction bearings, or "hotboxes." Oil-fired locomotives did not incur the delays of en route stops for coal, and the absence of a coal bunker simplified the task of fully streamlining the tender. So perfectly matched was the streamlining that the tender resembled the trailing cars more than it did a crucial adjunct to the engine.

The *Hiawathas'* cars were every bit as remarkable as their locomotives. Although roughly 40 percent lighter than the typical heavyweight cars then in service, the fact that they remained heavier than the new crop of "extremely light weight" articulated cars was portrayed as a definite comfort and safety virtue.

Designed under the direction of Milwaukee Road chief mechanical officer Karl Nystrom, they were the progenitors of several generations of innovative and idiosyncratic passenger cars built at the railroad's own West Milwaukee shops. The cars rode on modern four-wheel trucks of Nystrom's own design. The smoothly welded, low-profile carbodies with their bright, boldly striped paint scheme embodied the stark—almost sterile—streamlined esthetic, even if their narrow and slightly arched windows harked back to earlier tastes in car architecture.

As inaugurated, each six-car train carried a tap-diner (with a "Tip Top Tap" room marking the debut of cocktail bars aboard American trains), three coaches, a parlor car, and a parlor-observation car.

The two new *Hiawatha* consists were punctuated by observation cars that would gain celebrity on a par with the trains' locomotives. Eschewing the "boat-tailed" round-ended observation car profile established in 1933 by the Pullman Company's experimental *George M. Pullman* and embraced by contemporary *Zephyrs* and Union Pacific *Streamliners*, Nystrom's team created and christened the "Beaver Tail," perhaps best described as a shovel-nose in retreat. Small, curved rear-end windows and inward-facing seating combined to make the "observation" value of the cars somewhat doubtful, but they became icons nonetheless.

By the end of the *Hiawathas'* first summer, traffic levels had resulted in two more coaches being added to each consist, along with an express car—demonstrating a key advantage held by conventional, coupled consists over articulated, fixed-consist rivals like the Burlington *Zephyrs*. Barely five months after their debut, the *Hiawathas* had carried 100,000 passengers and established themselves as a force to be reckoned with in the hotly contested Chicago–Twin Cities market. Over the two months of June and July 1935, the *Hiawathas* carried

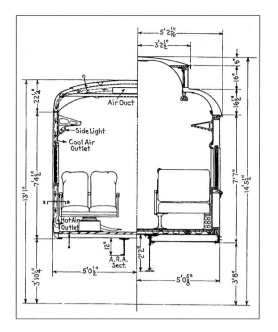

This cross section demonstrates the much lower profile of the 1935 *Hiawatha* cars as compared to older equipment. RAILWAY AGE

Floor plans depicting, top to bottom, the 1935 *Hiawatha's* coach, tap room-diner, parlor, and "Beaver Tail" parlor observation cars. RAILWAY AGE

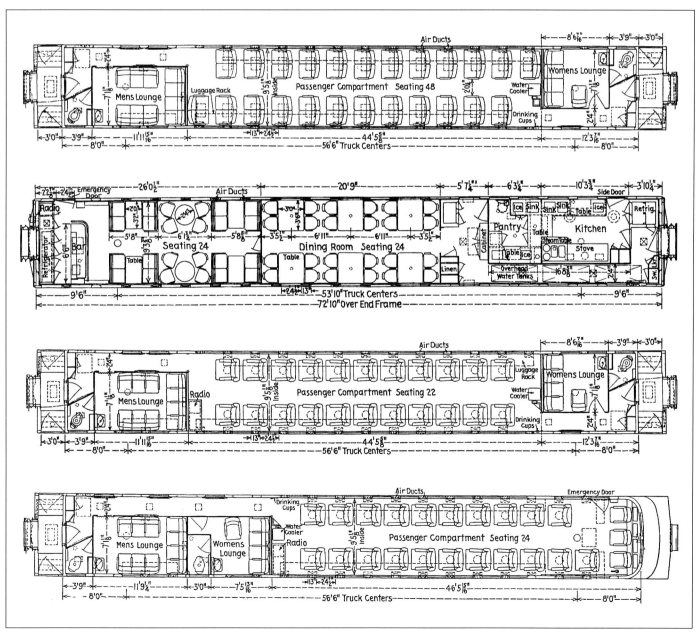

ABOVE: Class A No. 2 leads First 100, the eastbound *Afternoon Hiawatha*, at Minneapolis on September 2, 1935. ROBERT B. GRAHAM; TLC PUBLISHING COLLECTION

RIGHT: No. 2 again with an eastbound *Hiawatha*, this time crossing the Mississippi River via the "Short Line" bridge between Minneapolis and St. Paul on August 23, 1935. ROBERT B. GRAHAM; TLC PUBLISHING COLLECTION

INSET: The strong performance of the Milwaukee Roads' *Hiawathas* bolstered Alco's case for further development in streamlined steam. AUTHOR'S COLLECTION

35,376 passengers (a 290-per-trip average); gross revenues for the period were $188,610 against direct operating expenses of just $61,314.

On the last day of March 1936, well before their first birthday, the Milwaukee steamliners marked the carriage of their 200,000th fare, all the while having made inroads on bus, automobile, and rail competition. The trains celebrated their first anniversary with the announcement that they had earned the Milwaukee Road a profit of close to $700,000—not bad for the third horse to enter a three-horse race, and in the depths of the Depression, at that.

The trains had carried almost 250,000 paying passengers in their first year of operation, and the anniversary was marked with Native American-themed publicity at both end-points. In the May 29 Chicago celebration, 15 members of the Mohawk and Winnebago tribes in full dress traveled to Union Station—by

canoe, on the adjacent Chicago River—built a ceremonial fire in the train shed, and embraced the crew of Class A No. 2 as honorary tribe members. Pure 1930s kitsch, perhaps, but it ensured the *Hiawathas* a place in the headlines that only two days before had covered rival CB&Q's *Zephyr* fleet's millionth mile.

Through the end of August 1936, the *Hiawathas* had carried 323,585 passengers since their debut. In that one summer month, traffic aboard the trains was 36% heavier than during the same period in 1935. The milestone of the 500,000th *Hiawatha* passenger was reached on March 19, 1937.

Two more Class A 4-4-2s, numbered 3 and 4, arrived from Schenectady in May 1936 and April 1937, respectively. Large, stylized images of "Hiawatha" were added to all four locomotives' tender flanks (only No. 4 was delivered that way). The arrival

of Nos. 3 and 4 meant that the streamlined Atlantics could be seen with regularity on Chicago–Milwaukee runs, among others.

In the summer of 1936, to foster a family appearance in the *Hiawatha's* new seasonal New Lisbon–Star Lake (Wis.) "North Woods" connection, some remarkable sleight-of-hand was performed by the magicians at Milwaukee shops. A 36-year-old 4-6-0, built by Baldwin in October 1900, was transformed into a cosmetic twin of the celebrated Class A

Atlantics. With its Ten-Wheeler running gear partially concealed by skirting, No. 10's non-vestibule cab and its squat tender were the only tip-offs to the casual observer. Unlike the Atlantics, No. 10 (and its 1937 twin, No. 11—built in September 1900 as a Class B-3) were coal-fired, with a 12-ton, 8,500-gallon tender barely long enough to accommodate THE MILWAUKEE ROAD lettering. Nos. 10 and 11 were designated Class G upon their streamlined metamorphosis.

Two veteran Ten-Wheelers were shrouded by Milwaukee shops in 1936 and 1937 to emulate the Class A Atlantics. Numbered 10 and 11, they were assigned to the *Hiawatha's* "North Woods" connection. No. 11 rested at New Lisbon, Wis., in August 1940. Unlike their larger cousins, Nos. 10 and 11 were coal burners.
HAROLD K. VOLLRATH COLLECTION

Class G Ten-Wheeler No. 10 was at New Lisbon, Wis., on June 28, 1937. This engine was built by Baldwin in 1900 as a Vauclain compound and converted to a simple, superheated configuration by the railroad in 1926.
JAY WILLIAMS COLLECTION

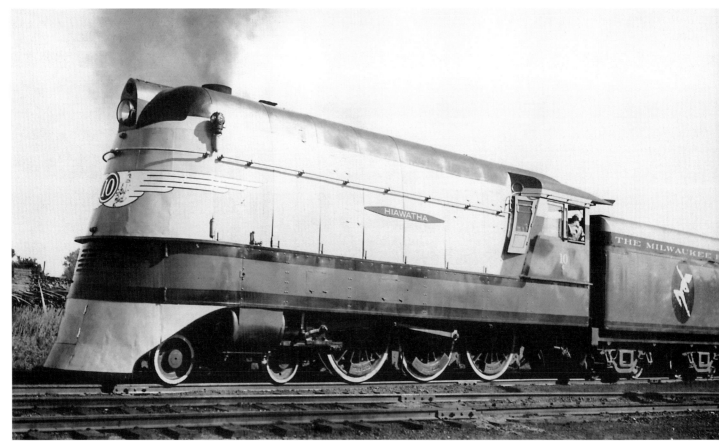

On October 11, 1936, following a week of on-line public display, the second generation of *Hiawatha* rolling stock was placed in service.

The all-new home-built cars—dubbed "The *Hiawatha* of 1937" by the railroad—incorporated a number of evolutionary improvements over their predecessors. Readily apparent were the horizontal ribs above and below the windows, marking the debut of a Milwaukee Road styling trait that would eventually appear on freight cars and cabooses as well. Drag-inducing and visually cluttering underbody equipment on each car was concealed inside a steel box running along the full length of the center sill between the trucks. This arrangement also had the effect of lowering the cars' center of gravity by about seven inches. Square windows, full-width diaphragms, and a revised paint scheme were among the other more obvious changes in the new *Hiawatha* equipment.

The trains now included a full dining car, since the popular Tip Top Tap beverage room had been expanded to occupy half of the head-end combination car. One of the new parlor cars contained a drawing room, capable of accommodating up to seven passengers in privacy. The Beaver Tails were back, with more glass in their redesigned rear ends, but observation-room seating still faced inward.

Considerable weight reduction in the new cars enabled the original Atlantics to

maintain the same demanding 6.5-hour Chicago–Twin Cities schedule with a nine-car "1937" *Hiawatha* consist as they had with the earlier seven-car edition. The entire nine-car train weighed roughly 27 tons more than the seven-car consist, but offered 291 revenue seats against its predecessor's 238. Weight per seat was

The 1937 re-equipping of the *Hiawathas* introduced the rib-sided styling that would become a hallmark of the Milwaukee Road's home-built passenger cars. A full diner appeared, and the popular "Tip Top Tap" room was moved to the rear half of the first car. BOTH, JAY WILLIAMS COLLECTION

A Class A in full flight meets the competition as it leads a re-equipped "1937" *Hiawatha* over U.S. Route 41 at Gurnee, Illinois. A modified paint scheme and a horizontal rib above and below the windows denoted the 1937 cars. TLC PUBLISHING COLLECTION

markedly lower—almost 14 percent—in the new consists. While the original *Hiawatha* cars of 1935 weighed on the order of one-third less than conventional heavyweight equipment, the second-generation *Hiawathas* were roughly ten percent lighter still, weighing a remarkable

41 to 43 percent less than comparable heavyweight cars.

With the Milwaukee Road hard-pressed to keep up with passenger demand, new locomotives and even more new cars were on the *Hiawathas'* horizon. These are described in Chapter 3.

Battle-scarred Class A No. 2 displayed 15 years' worth of subtle changes at Milwaukee in September 1950. Stainless steel wings have been clipped, and numberboards, a Mars signal light, and additional pilot grills are among the additions. No. 2 was retired exactly one year later, along with No. 1. Younger siblings Nos. 3 and 4 left the roster in September 1949 and June 1951, respectively.
HAROLD K. VOLLRATH COLLECTION

FACING PAGE: Floor plans of the 1937 Hiawatha. RAILWAY AGE

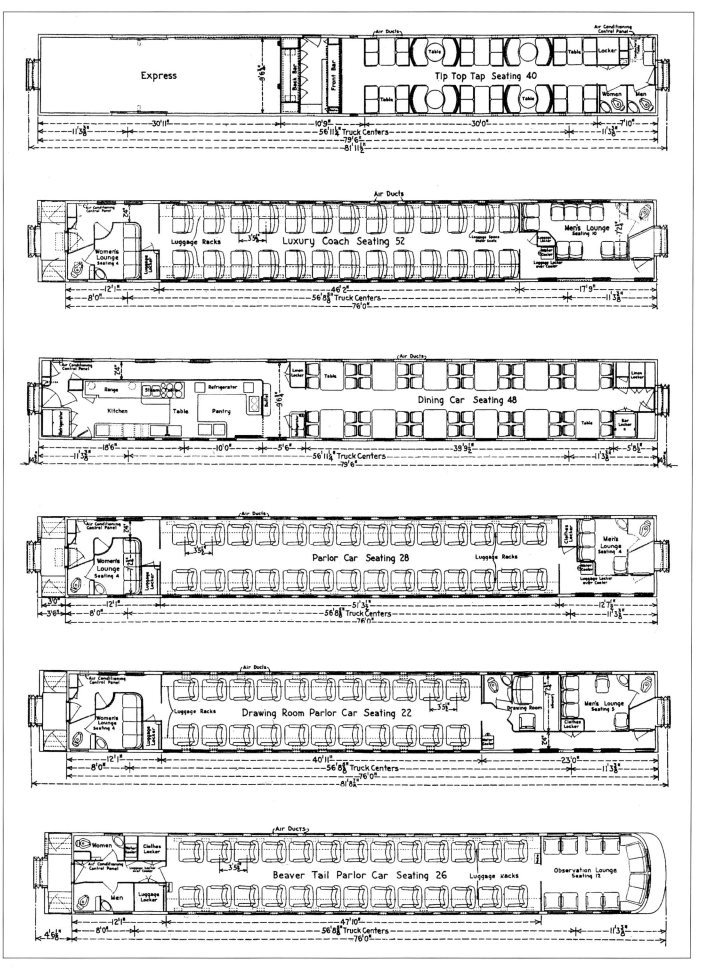

39

New York Central 2-8-2 Mohawk No. 2873 shows off the special streamlined shroud applied for duty at the head of the *Rexall Train* in 1936. The black, blue, and white locomotive was at Chicago Union Station on August 3, 1936. The shroud was removed at the conclusion of the train's extensive national tour, organized to take the place of the United Drug Company's traditional convention.
TLC PUBLISHING COLLECTION

THE REXALL TRAIN

A near-duplicate of the New York Central's *Commodore Vanderbilt* shrouding applied by the railroad to L-2 Mohawk No. 2873 in early 1936 had nothing to do with the "Great Steel Fleet."

Instead of bringing delegates to a national convention in 1936, the United Drug Company took the convention to its representatives in the form of the *Rexall Train*, a 12-car rolling showroom that travelled across the United States for seven months that year.

Visitors were presented with displays of the latest Rexall products along with mockups of the latest in drug store and soda fountain merchandising ideas. United Drug employees staffing the train were accommodated in standard Pullman sleeping cars, and also had on-board lounge and dining facilities—and even a dance floor—at their disposal.

The New York Central 4-8-2 leased to pull the heavyweight train was converted to burn oil (in deference to its nationwide assignment) and given a streamlined, blue, black, and white shroud for the duration of its special duty. The *Commodore's* streamlined contours were faithfully duplicated in elongated form, with then tender's roofline raised to match the balloon-roofed heavyweight cars in profile and contour. New York Central gained national exposure through a nose-mounted cast-metal monogram and rather discrete tender lettering, while THE REXALL TRAIN lettering adorned the broad white band above the engine's drivers.

THE MERCURY

New York Central took its own interest in streamlined trains to a higher level in late 1935, when the railroad began planning improvements to its Detroit–Toledo–Cleveland services. Traffic expectations on the 164-mile route dictated a "conventional" consist, as opposed to one of the burgeoning generation of limited-capacity, articulated, lightweight trainsets. Diesel-electric locomotives capable of reliably handling such a full-sized train on the required two hour, 50 minute schedule were, at best, still in the teething stage, so, as had been the case on the Milwaukee Road, steam got the nod for assignment to the new trains.

Drawing on ancient mythology—as the Burlington Route had done with its *Zephyrs*—NYC selected the name *Mercury* in a bid to convey the speed and reliability of its new service.

NYC President Fred Williamson turned to New York-based Henry Dreyfuss to design the new train, the first time one of the new crop of industrial designers had been tapped by an American railroad for such an all-encompassing commission. Dreyfuss' proposal for all-new equipment was initially approved by the railroad but was abruptly shelved when quotes came back from the commercial carbuilders.

Dreyfuss related in his 1955 book, *Designing for People*, how, en route to the suburbs aboard a NYC train and passing through the railroad's Mott Haven coach yards in the Bronx after the sudden cancellation of his proposal, he noticed a number of apparently stored commuter coaches. Dreyfuss proceeded to make a persuasive case to President Williamson that surplus cars such as these be rebuilt in-house to create the new train—thus meeting his client's needs and saving his commission. Costs proved to be only about one-quarter of what was demanded by the commercial builders, and the *Mercury* was born.

The ten-year-old commuter cars' smooth, arched roofs lent an already streamlined profile, and Dreyfuss incorporated deep underbody skirting, folding vestibule steps, full-width diaphragms, and strong horizontal styling elements on his ersatz streamliner. A subdued gray was the train's signature exterior color, but the window area of each car—with the original small, squared openings retained—was accented with aluminum paint and framed with brushed metal trim. Dreyfuss'

efforts were quite effective, although the cars' small windows and riveted construction gave away the secret upon more than a cursory inspection. One of the former Putnam Division commuter coaches underwent some remarkable cosmetic surgery at Central's Beech Grove (Indianapolis) shops to become the *Mercury's* signature car, the round-ended, deep-windowed parlor-observation *Detroit*. The treatment of the car's sloping, faceted rear glazing bore an uncanny resemblance to that proposed in 1931 by Norman Bel Geddes for his conceptual "Rear Lounge Car No. 4." An illuminated train-name tail-sign punctuated *Detroit's* observation end.

If the *Mercury* cars' exterior streamlining was, in many respects, a cost-driven compromise—that was, after all, how the project had been resuscitated—Dreyfuss' innovative interiors were stunningly modern by any

One of the two K-5a Pacifics styled by Henry Dreyfuss for the New York Central's 1936 *Mercury* stretched its legs at Beech Grove shops near Indianapolis prior to the train's July 15 inauguration.
NYC PHOTOS; NYCSHS COLLECTION

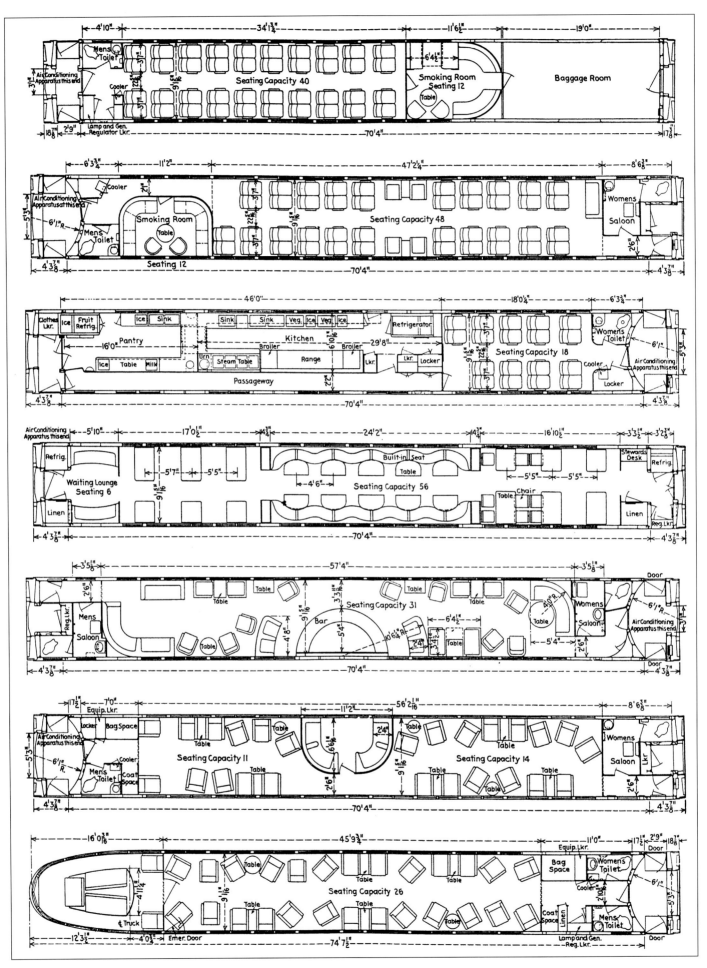

standards, and foretold what was up his sleeve for a future NYC commission. With Dreyfuss' designs to guide them, NYC's Engineering Department and Beech Grove shop forces gutted seven commuter cars and rebuilt them to baggage-coach, coach, coach-kitchen, full diner, lounge, parlor, and parlor-observation floor plans. The original seven-car consist provided 107 revenue coach seats and 57 revenue Pullman parlor seats. A remarkable 127 non-revenue seats were divided among two coach smoking lounges (24 seats), the 56-seat diner with its six-seat waiting alcove, the 31-seat Pullman-operated lounge car, and the ten-seat observation lounge. NYC proudly hailed the latter as the first in which the seats faced out instead of in.

The adoption of a full diner—with kitchen and pantry in an adjacent car—was dictated by the train's schedule and relatively short run. As originally carded, the westbound *Mercury* left Cleveland at 7:30 am, with 9:15 am and 10:20 am arrivals at Toledo and Detroit, respective-

ly. Passengers would expect breakfast, and would need to be served quickly but without feeling rushed. A similar situation, but over the dinner hours, existed eastbound, with the *Mercury* leaving Detroit at 5:35 pm, arriving in Toledo at 6:35 pm, and tieing up at Cleveland at 8:25 pm (original eastbound timing was 55 minutes later at all three stations on Sundays).

Unconstrained by the conventions of railroad car interior design, Dreyfuss sought to open up often claustrophobic interior confines while at the same time eliminating what he described as "the appearance of a well-tilled cabbage patch" inside contemporary coaches, parlors, and diners. His radical "rotunda" treatment, with wider-than-normal openings between cars connecting semi-circular vestibules, at once eliminated the cramped boxiness of the traditional vestibule while creating the impression that the entire consist was one interconnected unit rather than the series of independent cars which it in fact was. Dreyfuss' placement of planters, mirrors, partitions,

THE TRAIN OF TOMORROW
CUSTOM-BUILT
STREAMLINED
AIR CONDITIONED
Serving Detroit—Toledo—Cleveland

FACING PAGE: Floor plans of the original seven *Mercury* cars, designed by Henry Dreyfuss. RAILWAY AGE

Beech Grove's rebuilding of the seven former NYC Putnam Division commuter cars for the original *Mercury* included the remarkable conversion of one into the glass-ended observation car *Detroit*. NYC PHOTO; NYCSHS COLLECTION

One of the *Mercury's* two shrouded K-5a Pacifics posed at Beech Grove on May 15, 1936.

FACING PAGE, TOP AND MIDDLE: These two shop views reveal something of a *Mercury* Pacific's heritage— the K-5a hidden beneath the streamlined shroud. The boiler and smokebox cowling was attached to a steel framework supported by the running board.

FACING PAGE, BOTTOM: The *Mercury* Pacifics' drivers were painted aluminum and black. In a bit of machine-age theater, they were illuminated at night by three spotlights mounted under each running board. ALL NYC PHOTOS; NYCSHS COLLECTION

bar, lounge, and parlor compartment areas—coupled with his fresh use of color, texture, and lighting—broke the cars' interiors into cozy but still spacious segments and avoided the "tunnel" effect.

New York Central had sent a pair of 1926-vintage K-5a Pacifics, Nos. 4915 and 4917, to West Albany for rebuilding as *Mercury* power. Dreyfuss gave the Pacifics an evolutionary restyling of the *Commodore Vanderbilt's* bathtub shroud, painted medium gray with aluminum accents to match the *Mercury* cars. A considerably lowered headlight made the *Mercury* engines' shrouding appear to be more of a departure from the *Commodore's* than it actually was, but Dreyfuss' masterstroke was his emphasis of the *Mercury* Pacifics' refitted 79-inch Boxpok drivers. The designer created a remarkable bit of machine-age theater by superimposing a bold, black circle on each aluminum-painted driver, framing the drivers and rods in a close-cropped opening in the deep skirts that obscured the rest of the running gear, and illuminating the whole affair at night with spotlights mounted under the running boards.

Lettering on the locomotives was kept to a minimum, with just an NYC oval monogram on the nose below the headlight, THE MERCURY name below the cab windows, and the NEW YORK CENTRAL roadname high on the sides of each tender. Conspicuous in their absence were the locomotives' road numbers, which were later added below the cab windows to augment their original but normally unseen location on the rear of the tenders. All lettering was rendered in aluminum paint, and brushed metal trim was used to accent the pilot, skirt edges, and tender.

Like the *Commodore Vanderbilt*, the *Mercury* locomotives' tenders were streamlined with fully enclosed coal bunkers. Tenders matched the trailing cars in profile and cross-section. Ohio Brass (O-B) tight-lock couplers with integral steam, air, and electrical connections were employed throughout the train, and augmented conventional steam, air, and signal lines applied to the tenders for maximum interchangeability.

Promotion of the *Mercury* and its futuristic locomotives began even before the train's inauguration. A highlight was the side-by-side "passing of the torch"

The *Mercury* was christened during June 25, 1936, ceremonies at Indianapolis Union Station. The location was not on the train's intended route, but paid tribute to nearby Beech Grove shops.
NYC PHOTO; NYCSHS COLLECTION

The *Mercury*'s immediate popularity dictated that additional cars be added to the original seven-car consist. This eight-car edition sped westbound behind No. 4917 near Sandusky, Ohio, in July 1938 on its way to Detroit. The train's longer consists taxed the streamlined Pacifics—and precipitated their reassignment to the *James Whitcomb Riley*. Note the bright metal trim added atop the running board skirt.
A. HIRZ; NYCSHS COLLECTION

For all the *Mercury* Pacifics' external modernity, the interiors of their cabs were thoroughly traditional. NYC PHOTO; NYCSHS COLLECTION

between Hudson No. 5255 and streamlined No. 4915 on May 15, 1936. With motion picture and still cameras recording the event, the two locomotives—the Hudson, ironically, the younger of the two—paced each other along the Hudson south of Harmon, New York.

The original seven-car *Mercury* consist was christened at Indianapolis Union Station—off its intended route but honoring Beech Grove's role in its creation—on June 25, 1936. The *Mercury's* streamlined steam locomotive was center stage at the ceremony when Louise Landman, the daughter of NYC's General Passenger Traffic Manager, broke a bottle of Ohio champagne over the engine's sleek pilot. Following the festivities, the *Mercury* was sent back east to New York City for public exhibition at Grand Central Terminal on June 28 and 29.

A press trip out of Cleveland Union Terminal on July 13 built regional interest in NYC's "Train of Tomorrow"—a title that would be recycled on several occasions over the ensuing two decades as American railroads sought to lure passengers away from the competition's siren songs. The *Mercury* commenced revenue service two days later, on July 15, 1936.

The wisdom of employing a non-articulated consist was soon evident, as passenger demand often exceeded the original seven-car train's capacity. Two more matching coaches, converted at Beech Grove later in 1936, proved a mixed blessing, though, as the heavier consists taxed the 37,600-pound tractive force of the streamlined Pacifics.

At the end of the *Mercury's* first year of service, NYC reported that ridership on its Cleveland–Detroit route had increased by more than 100%.

A second trainset of matching rebuilt cars emerged from Beech Grove in 1939, by which time the *Mercury's* route had been extended west to Chicago and the heavier trains were routinely powered by NYC's more powerful Hudsons. The two Dreyfuss-styled Pacifics were transferred back to their original home territory on NYC's "Big Four" subsidiary in 1939. They became the regular power on the streamlined, all-coach *James Whitcomb Riley* between Cincinnati, Indianapolis, and Chicago's lakefront Central Station. In this service, the two Pacifics retained their gray *Mercury* shrouding, but with revised tender paint and JAMES WHITCOMB RILEY lettering below the cab windows, and bug-eye classification lamps—a Big Four standard—flanking the nose-top air intake grill. The *Riley* is discussed in greater detail in Chapter 4

Mr. Loewy Goes to Altoona

Fresh from his 1934 finessing of the Pennsylvania Railroad's already streamlined GG1 electric into a welded-carbody, pinstriped legend, Raymond Loewy was given the task of streamlining one of the Pennsy's ubiquitous K-4s Pacifics.

This class of locomotives, 424 strong at its zenith, had been designed in 1914 as a more powerful development of the Pennsy's successful Class E-6s Atlantics. Eighty E-6s Atlantics had been built to a 1910 PRR design, but heavier passenger trains required a locomotive with even greater tractive force and high-speed horsepower. That requirement led to the design of the K-4s, and the class became the backbone of the Pennsy's steam passenger stable.

A 1920 product of the railroad's Altoona (Pa.) works, 80-inch-drivered 4-6-2 No. 3768 emerged from its March 1936 makeover to become the Pennsylvania's—and Loewy's—first streamlined steam locomotive.

Following wind tunnel research at New York University, Loewy broke from U.S. precedent and adopted a torpedo-nosed treatment sculpted around, rather than completely concealing, the two main

LEFT: Its Altoona facelift just completed and with a dozen heavyweight coaches in tow, Pennsylvania K4s No. 3768 makes an early evaluation trip in March 1936.
PRR PHOTO; AUTHOR'S COLLECTION

FACING PAGE, BOTTOM: The converging angles of No. 3768's smoke-lifting elements are apparent in this March 5, 1936, view. Loewy's streamlined K4s was posed alongside unshrouded classmate No. 3847. PRR PHOTO; JAY WILLIAMS COLLECTION

BELOW: By the time of this April 16, 1936, portrait No. 3768's winged keystone had been modified and relocated to the hemispherical nose. In the weeks ahead an estimated 300,000 people would visit the streamlined K4s as it toured the railroad.
PRR PHOTO; AUTHOR'S COLLECTION

A fireman's-side view of No. 3768, at Pittsburgh on April 20, 1938. J. R. QUINN COLLECTION

structural elements of the Pacific's front end—the smokebox and pilot. The design ultimately adopted was one of 28 variations tested in the wind tunnel, in one of the first such uses of clay styling models. Aerodynamic effects were rendered visible by silk threads attached to the models, and by smoke added to the air flow. Employment of a wind tunnel in locomotive design was not new, though. Canadian National begun its pioneering work in Ottawa in 1931, with the results widely published in the North American railroad trade press during 1933 (see Chapter 5).

The winning PRR design, abandoning a shovel nose in favor of Loewy's more sculpted profile, minimized low-pressure waves above and adjacent to the boiler, and thus improved the exhaust flow. An integral arrangement of converging planes atop the boiler, behind the smoke stack, was intended to lift the engine's exhaust well above the cab.

Even though Loewy's streamlined shroud was more "form-fitting" than its New York Central and Milwaukee Road antecedents, it still managed to conceal all of the locomotive's piping, domes, and assorted linkages.

No. 3768 emerged from Altoona in dark gunmetal paint, with gold tender lettering and striping. A narrow stripe curving around the cab windows was also gold, but stainless steel was used for the remaining engine striping as well as for the handrails and the winged PRR keystone on the front of the stack (this latter detail was soon moved down to a position on the hemispherical smokebox fairing, above the headlight).

In what was becoming common practice, a vestibule-type cab and rubber gasket helped conceal the break between engine and tender. Loewy embraced style over practicality by dropping the engine's running gear skirts down to match the height of the tender's side sill. This restricted ready access to parts of the running gear, but the removal of a few bolts released much of the aluminum skirting to permit in-depth inspection and shop work. Running inspections were accommodated by strategically placed doors in the shrouding. The locomotive's clean front end was enhanced by the ability to completely conceal the coupler by folding it back behind a pilot panel.

Between June 19 and July 10, 1936, the locomotive was sent on a display tour of the PRR's Eastern Region. Over 101,000 people came to see this harbinger of Pennsy's "Fleet of Modernism" during an

initial 11-city circuit that included Altoona, Reading, Pottsville, Wilkes Barre, Sunbury, Williamsport, Lock Haven, Renova, Lancaster, York (all in Pennsylvania), and Elmira, New York. So powerful was the allure of railroading's "new look" that another 200,000 of the curious clamored to see No. 3768 in the ensuing weeks at 24 more Midwestern display stops. In the interim, the locomotive was put through its paces at the head of Pennsy's finest trains, chief among them the flagship *Broadway Limited*. Its big moment in the spotlight, however, was still two years in the future.

SPEEDING BULLETS

Loewy's sculptured treatment of No. 3768—evoking the earlier torpedo-silhouetted proposals of Otto Kuhler—marked a turning point in the appearance of American streamlined steam. More and more railroads would forsake the "bathtub" style of shrouding and instead give their steam locomotives a more form-fitting cloak.

Although the combination of shovel nose and generously shrouded components would continue to find favor with some streamlined steam practitioners, the configuration's real future lay else-

where—with the diesel-electric builders. The path had been established with the Burlington *Zephyrs*, with a lineage back to the mechanically unsuccessful Michelin railcar assembled by Budd in 1933 for the Texas & Pacific.

Beyond the "glamor" of the new articulated streamliners, though, the 1936 retrofit of a shovel nose to B&O No. 50 was a clear signal that streamlining would embrace the coming generation of individual-unit diesel-electrics, as well. The industrial designers already knew this, and Electro-Motive's stylists produced several futuristic renderings for Santa Fe.

It was left to Electro-Motive to perfect the form—in conjunction with an order for B&O, as it happened—on the group of EA model passenger diesels built in 1937 and 1938. These were the first of the legendary "E-units," and were soon followed by E1s for Santa Fe. The shovel-nosed, full-width carbody applied to these units was clean of line and smooth of contour—there was a bit of Loewy's GG-1 in this handsome mutt. Had it been applied to a steam locomotive, though, it would have been called one thing—a bathtub.

For streamlined steam in North America, the formative years were over. It was show time.

Running-gear shrouding on streamlined steam was the bane of the mechanical and operating departments, and most subsequent designs would not repeat the deep skirting specified by Loewy for PRR No. 3768. It was ultimately removed, as was the upper plane of the smoke-lifting apparatus.
J. R. QUINN COLLECTION

3 MOMENTUM

Santa Fe's "Blue Goose," streamlined Hudson No. 3460, is flanked by Electro-Motive E1s during a display of the railway's latest passenger equipment at Chicago's Dearborn Station in 1938. E1 No. 6, at right, leads the *El Capitan*. J. MICHAEL GRUBER COLLECTION

By the beginning of 1937, streamlined trains were firmly established as the wave of the future on America's railroads. A streamlined locomotive—whether steam, electric, or diesel—was still all a railroad needed to make headlines and attract crowds, even if its trailing cars were unstreamlined throwbacks to earlier times.

Larger and more powerful diesel-electric locomotives were appearing on passenger trains throughout the country, and their Electro-Motive Corporation designers had bestowed them with the brightly painted, streamlined carbodies that passengers and railroad sales staff alike had come to expect.

Several influential roads, however—large and not so large—still considered steam superior in terms of speed, reliability, serviceability, and cost.

The next couple of years would see the inauguration of some of the finest and most famous streamlined passenger train consists ever to operate in America. With the diesel-electric's star rapidly rising, the closing years of the 1930s would witness the zenith of streamlined steam. War and economics would intervene all too soon and accelerate the already rapid pace of change within the railroad industry.

For a brief period, however, the steamliners reigned supreme.

THE SUN RISES IN THE WEST

Streamlined steam in the United States remained an Eastern and Midwestern phenomenon until March 21, 1937, when Southern Pacific launched its *Daylights* on the Coast Line between Los Angeles and San Francisco.

The Lima Locomotive Works got SP's nod to design and build a group of six Class GS-2 Northerns (Nos. 4410-4415) for the new *Daylights*. The curving, hilly route dictated 4-8-4 power for the new trains,

Southern Pacific No. 4416 posed at its Ohio builder in 1937. This Class GS-3 locomotive was the first in SP's second order for *Daylight* power, and introduced a number of improvements over the earlier GS-2 class, Nos. 4410-4415.
TLC PUBLISHING COLLECTION

SP Class GS-2 No 4414, at San Mateo, California, on March 22, 1941, exhibited the original *Daylight* locomotives' smaller 73.5-inch drivers and shorter wheelbase. Differences in boiler pressure, cylinders, weight, and tractive force were less apparent.
J. R. QUINN COLLECTION

combining the ability to maintain a considerably tightened schedule over the 471-mile line's numerous grades (of up to 2.2%) with the "legs" to race over straighter, level segments. The previous, heavyweight edition of the *Daylight*—the name dated to 1922—took 12.5 hours to make the Los Angeles–San Francisco trip, but the combination of lightweight cars and new 4-8-4s cut this to just nine hours and 45 minutes with the debut of the 1937 train. The acceleration of the *Daylight's* schedule was one of the more visible examples of a system-wide tightening of SP passenger train timings in the mid-1930s.

New equipment was only part of the equation enabling the *Daylight's* speed. Substantial trackwork was undertaken on Southern Pacific's Coast Route, with close to 80 track-miles of heavier rail and over 100 miles of improved ballast installed. A number of curves were eased, as well, before the streamlined *Daylight* turned a revenue wheel.

Lima billed its first streamlined steam as the largest and most powerful such locomotives yet created, and the new Southern Pacific "Golden State" class was well-represented in the builder's trade advertising during the late 1930s.

GS-2 Northerns Nos. 4410-4415 weighed 448,400 pounds (exclusive of their tenders), with 266,500 pounds on their 73.5-inch drivers. With 250 PSI steam pressure and 27x30-inch cylinders, they could exert 62,200 pounds of tractive force, or an impressive 74,710 pounds with the trailing-truck booster cut in. Their 12-wheel tenders carried 22,000 gallons of water and 6,275 gallons of fuel oil. Total engine and tender length was 94.5 feet. These were, indeed, big engines.

Their exterior styling was, at best, semi-streamlined, with paint going farther than sheet metal in creating the GS' enduring mystique.

The two main streamlining elements employed were a full-length skyline casing and deep running board skirts. A non-retractable coupler jutted out of the smooth, chrome-trimmed pilot. The area above the pilot was left open, graced only

"Streamstyled" rather than truly streamlined, Southern Pacific's GS-class Northerns showed how effective a well-executed paint scheme could be when used in conjunction with minimal sheet metal shrouding. GS-2 No. 4412 blended with its trailing *Daylight* consist at Los Angeles following a pre-inaugural run in March 1937. SP used the indicators at the front of the skyline casing to display train numbers. Train No. 99 was the northbound *Daylight*.
SP PHOTO; JOE SCHMITZ COLLECTION

GS-2 No. 4420 led a *Daylight* at Santa Susana, California, in 1940. JOE SCHMITZ COLLECTION

by the bell and a small cast-metal numberboard. The aluminum-painted smokebox front displayed its bolts and hinges for the world to see, but the manner in which the single, centered headlight—flanked by small illuminated numberboards—was faired into the smaller of two smokebox doors lent a purposeful, bullet-nosed effect. An angled train number indicator was mounted on either side of the skyline casing's front end, above and just aft of a pair of teardrop-shaped aluminum marker light fixtures. The flared bell of a Typhon air horn protruded from the front of the skyline. The traditional steam-operated whistle was concealed in a well atop the casing.

The color scheme developed for the *Daylight* was stunning. The pilot and running board skirting established a broad orange stripe the trailed back across the tender in line with the passenger cars' window band. A narrower red stripe erupted from the side of the boiler to form a line matching the cars' letterboard height, and a similarly colored panel flared below the orange band on the tender. This led into the red-painted lower sides of the *Daylight* consist. (SP was one of a small group of railroads opting over the years to paint the sides of their stainless steel-clad cars). The balance of the locomotive and tender was painted black.

Use of a vestibule-type cab on Classes GS-4 and GS-5 helped carry the color bands between engine and tender with a minimum of disruption.

The *Daylight's* stylized signature emblem, a winged sun with the train's name in flowing script, was applied to the forward portion of the running board skirt and also appeared on the side of each car. Narrow aluminum stripes separated the other colors. Lettering throughout the train's exterior was in aluminum paint.

Southern Pacific invested approximately $1 million apiece in the two 12-car *Daylight* consists. The Pullman-Standard cars, built of Cor-Ten steel and sheathed in stainless steel fluting, encompassed coach, coffee-shop, tavern-lounge, diner, parlor, and parlor-observation floor plans. Four-wheeled, triple-bolster trucks were designed to give a smooth ride, while *de rigeur* tight-lock couplers took care of any slack action.

The *Daylight* needed just 135 days to reach the 100,000-passenger milestone; at the end of six months, the figure was 144,430, almost evenly split between northbound and southbound traffic. Close to 650,000 riders had been carried by the time of the *Daylight's* second birthday. So strong was ridership that two additional 14-car consists were ordered from P-S in 1939. These cars entered service on

Bringing up the rear of each *Daylight* was a round-ended Pullman-Standard parlor-observation car. Their interiors offered Southern Pacific passengers an Art Deco haven.
SP PHOTO; AUTHOR'S COLLECTION

A Class GS-3 leads a 14-car *Daylight* north along the Pacific coast from Los Angeles to San Francisco in 1940. The consist includes two twin-unit articulated coaches and a three-unit diner.
SP PHOTO; AUTHOR'S COLLECTION

January 5, 1940, and their arrival permitted the original *Daylight* cars to be temporarily withdrawn from service for refurbishing. They reappeared on March 30, 1940, as the *Noon Daylight*, at which time the two newer consists were reassigned as the *Morning Daylight* to offer double-daily service on the route. Other steam-powered *Daylights* followed, and the GS-class locomotives most often associated with the *Daylights* held assignments on other SP trains. These and other SP motive power developments are discussed in Chapter 4.

As powerful as the original six *Daylight* 4-8-4s were, they were eclipsed—if only slightly—by a further 14 locomotives delivered by Lima late in 1937 as SP Nos. 4416-4429. Classed GS-3, this group featured 80-inch drivers, an 18-inch-longer driver wheelbase and a 22-inch-longer total engine wheelbase, a maximum tractive

Fresh from Lima, No. 4450—the first of SP's second batch of "warbaby" GS-4s—waited at Los Angeles on May 22, 1942, to begin its maiden trip on Train No. 99. The headlight visor is in reponse to the perceived threat of Japanese military activity on the California coast.
HAROLD K. VOLLRATH COLLECTION

GS-4 No. 4452 led the *Lark*, Train No. 75, into San Francisco in 1952. The train's two-tone gray livery was a mismatch to the locomotive's *Daylight* colors. Note the larger tender lettering, and the absence of pilot trim strips.
A. THOMSON; JOE SCHMITZ COLLECTION

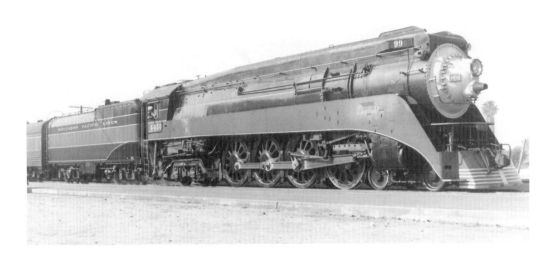

force of 74,710 pounds, an increased boiler pressure of 280 PSI, and cylinders one inch narrower in diameter. Despite their being 11,600 pounds heavier than the earlier *Daylight* locomotives, the weight on drivers of this second group was only 800 pounds higher, and the weight of reciprocating parts was markedly lighter. Tender capacities were identical, and streamlining and paint scheme mirrored the first group.

In Texas, meanwhile, the *Sunbeam* of SP subsidiary Texas & New Orleans (T&NO) became that state's first steamliner when it commenced revenue service between Dallas and Houston on September 19, 1937. Sixteen new lightweight cars were delivered by Pullman-Standard specifically for this service, in baggage, coach, parlor, and diner-lounge-observation floor plans. Each eight-car train could accommodate 326 revenue passengers. The car exteriors, although sheathed in stainless steel fluting, were given the same red-and-orange paint scheme as the parent's *Daylight* equipment.

Planned to provide a single daily trip in each direction between Dallas and Houston, the *Sunbeam* soon began running twice daily to meet demand, at which time the morning schedule was renamed the *Hustler*. Initial schedules allowed just 265 minutes for the 264-mile trip, in a market hotly contested by the diesel-powered Rock Island *Texas Rocket* and the Burlington's *Sam Houston Zephyr* (the lat-

ter was the reassigned *Pioneer Zephyr* articulated trainset of 1934). As had been the case with the *Daylight's* Coast Line route, substantial trackwork preceded the introduction of SP's Texas speedster.

Power for the new T&NO train was provided by a trio of Southern Pacific Class P-6 Pacifics dating back to 1913 and modernized in SP's Houston shops. Although they retained their decidedly unstreamlined Vanderbilt tenders, the transformation was still remarkable. Nos. 650-652 emerged as Class P-14—miniaturized versions of the *Daylight* 4-8-4s, even going their big brothers one better with the installation of a sheet metal fairing between pilot and smokebox and a smoother "bullet" nosecone. The rebuilt Pacifics' 77-inch Boxpok drivers conveyed 40,570 pounds of tractive force to the rails, and the reciprocating parts were balanced to permit the locomotives to achieve 100 MPH when necessary.

The trio of streamlined Pacifics held down the *Sunbeam/Hustler* assignment until the trains were dieselized in 1953. All three were scrapped the following year.

THE SHORE LINERS
The New York, New Haven & Hartford, a pioneer in the adoption of lightweight, streamstyled passenger cars and articulated trainsets, followed suit with a 1936 order to Baldwin for ten I-5 Class 4-6-4 Hudsons (Nos. 1400-1409).

The Houston, Texas, shops of Southern Pacific subsidiary Texas & New Orleans rebuilt three former SP Pacifics in 1937, giving them GS-like paint and streamlining for service on the Dallas–Houston *Sunbeam*. T&NO No. 650 leads Train No. 13 near Houston in June 1953, shortly before the *Sunbeam* and its running mate, the *Hustler*, had their P-14s replaced by diesels.
HAROLD K. VOLLRATH COLLECTION

The I-5 class was hailed by the New Haven as, "the *first* steam locomotives built along scientifically streamlined design for service on any eastern railroad." Hyperbole aside, they marked the largest-yet group of streamlined steam locomotives, Baldwin's first foray into the genre, and the first time that a group of U.S. streamlined steam locomotives had been created independently of a matching trainset (NYC's *Commodore Vanderbilt* and PRR 3768 notwithstanding—both of which had earned their keep primarily as evaluation and publicity instruments).

The New Haven's most recent steam passenger locomotives in late 1936 dated to the First World War, and heavy consists along the New Haven's busy "Shore Line"

Shop hands at Boston tend to New Haven "Shore Liner" No. 1404 in August 1938. The I-5 class was delivered with the railroad's name spelled out on the tender, but this was soon replaced by the New Haven's elaborate script monogram. EARLE G. BOYD; TLC PUBLISHING COLLECTION

The I-5 engines drew assignments on the New Haven's heavyweight limiteds—witness No. 1406 circa 1946. JAY WILLIAMS COLLECTION

between New Haven (Conn.) and Boston's South Station demanded correspondingly heavier power. A group of 50 Class I-4 Pacifics, built by Alco in 1916, bore the brunt of the New Haven's heavy passenger work through the 1920s and early 1930s, but even when double-headed were hard-pressed to maintain speed with more than a dozen cars over the 156.8-mile line's maximum 0.7 percent grade (a five-mile hill not far from Boston). Curvature was an even greater impediment to Shore Line schedules—the route negotiated the equivalent of nearly a dozen full circles between Boston and New Haven. Loco-motives were needed that could acceler-ate a 16-car consist quickly to recover from the 50 speed restrictions imposed by the route's curves and drawbridges.

In developing specifications for the new class of locomotives, two of the 1916-vintage I-4s were doubleheaded with a 12-car test train including a dynamometer car to measure their performance. With the objective of a single locomotive able to maintain a speed of at least 60 MPH up the Shore Line's ruling grade with a dozen passenger cars in tow, the I-4 test results provided the foundation of the new Hud-sons' design. Potential use of the new locomotives on the company's New Haven–Springfield (Mass.) route, with its somewhat lighter track structure, was also a design consideration. (East of New Haven, trains serving New York's Grand Central Terminal and Pennsylvania Sta-tion were hauled by electric power.)

The locomotives that ultimately emerged from the dynamometer charts and Baldwin's Eddystone (Pa.) plant weighed 193,000 pounds on drivers vs. 165,000 pounds for the venerable I-4. Other I-5 vs. I-4 comparisons: cylinders, 22x30 inches vs. 26x28; steam pressure, 285 PSI vs. 200 PSI; driver diameter, 80 inches vs. 79 inches; and tractive force, 44,000 pounds vs. 40,800 pounds.

The I-5s, dubbed the Shore Liner type by their owner, were given what *Railway Age* termed a "clean-cut" appearance. The railroad's own publicity was rather more effervescent: "The streamlined Shore Line type ... locomotives are patterned after modern high-speed rifle bullets—as you look at the one-unit cab and boiler you think of a speedlined bullet with the headlight forming the nose of the projec-tile." The 1937 booklet promoting the

Class I-5 No. 1401 charged through South Haven, Conn., in May 1940. J. R. QUINN COLLECTION

The New Haven got plenty of promotional mileage from its streamlined Hudsons, beginning with a die-cut booklet produced in 1937 (below) announcing their development and giving details of their design and construction. The I-5s' "projectile" profile also graced New Haven public timetables and travel brochures, among other items, over the years. BOTH, AUTHOR'S COLLECTION

"WE'LL BE BACK IN NEW HAVEN WITH A SEARCH WARRANT"

On March 3, 1937, in Boston, Baldwin Locomotive Works Vice-President Roberts S. Binkerd formally delivered the first Class I-5 streamlined Hudson to New Haven Railroad Vice-President and General Manager R. L. Pearson. During the South Station ceremony, Binkerd delivered a short address that gave an insight into the builder's philosophy—and the New Haven's—at a particularly turbulent time in motive power evolution. Binkerd's remarks appeared in the April 1937 issue of *Baldwin Locomotives*, the builder's company magazine, and are reprinted here:

Mr. Pearson, it gives me pleasure to turn over to you locomotive No. 1400, the first of a fleet of ten now on order. We are proud to be the builder of this locomotive, and hope that you will be the equally proud owner and user of it in the public service.

The improvement of your passenger service, outside of your electrified zone, you have wisely entrusted to steam locomotives. For considerably less than the cost of two fair-sized light-weight trains now so much talked about, you have acquired the means of improving the service of some thirty to forty trains a day.

Just last Sunday I was reading some contemporaneous accounts of the Baldwin-Westinghouse combination to design and build electric locomotives, made in 1895. Thanks to this combination, we have had the good fortune to build about two-thirds of the electric locomotives in this country, as well as many abroad. But the headline in the *Philadelphia Public Ledger* of August 6, 1895, read: "Steam Will Be Set Aside." Yet—speaking impartially as a builder of all forms of power—today, after forty-two years, the steam locomotive is a hotter competitor of the electric locomotive than ever before.

But the Iron Horse of today is not the Iron Horse of yesterday. In the locomotive now before you the liners on the pedestals fit into the grooves on the roller-bearing boxes with a tolerance of only 15 thousandths of an inch. Modern alloys are used to lighten rods and motion work. With a steam pressure of 285 lbs., it has nearly double the horsepower per ton of dead-weight of most of the locomotives of yesterday. Dollar for dollar, in first cost or in operating expenses, this modern steam locomotive of yours can show her heels to her counterpart in any other form of power. If you don't get 125,000 miles or more per year out of her, we'll be back in New Haven with a search warrant.

So take her, sir, and treat her kindly, and a most likely and lively wench she'll prove to be!

forthcoming locomotives continued, "With all of the working parts above the wheels concealed in the streamlining this modern New Haven locomotive cuts through air resistance with a minimum of friction—a maximum of speed."

Clean of line without, in fact, being fully streamlined—in the vein of SP's *Daylight* Northerns—each I-5 possessed a full-length skyline casing, a smooth pilot concealing a retractable coupler assembly, a sheet-metal fairing over the lower front end, and a conical smokebox front—"the nose of the projectile"—receding from the Golden Glow headlight. At the front of the skyline casing was a grilled air intake, the flow from which was exhausted aft of the stack as a smoke-lifting system. Beyond vestigial skirting ahead of the cylinders and below the cab, the I-5s' running gear was fully exposed. The running board edges were, however, accented with a six-inch-deep stainless steel strip that dipped below the cab in a shallow "S" and was continued across the sides and rear of the tender in aluminum paint. Handrails were clad in stainless steel, and two more stainless trim strips were applied across the pilot. The Shore Liners' Boxpok drivers, painted aluminum with a bold black circle, were an emulative nod to Dreyfuss' *Mercury* Pacifics of the previous year. Lettering was aluminum paint; the locomotive and tender were basic black.

Cabs were conventional—open to the elements at the rear—and no attempt was made to conceal the space between engine and tender. The stoker-equipped, 12-wheel tenders held 16 tons of coal and 18,000 gallons of water.

The first I-5 was ceremonially delivered during a March 3, 1937, gathering at Boston's South Station, after No. 1400 had led a VIP train along the scenic Shore Line from New Haven. Baldwin Vice-President Robert S. Binkerd presented the class engine to Robert L. Pearson, the New Haven's Vice-President and General Manager, with a short address that reflected on the I-5s' advances over past generations of steam and their practicality when compared to contemporary lightweight trainsets—with which the New Haven had been, and would continue to be, closely involved (see sidebar at left).

The first I-5 entered revenue service on March 28, 1937, and all were on the job by May 8. The Shore Liners were every bit the powerhouses sought by the New Haven, managing a top timing of just two hours and 51 minutes with the two-stop *Merchants Limited* over the 156.8 miles between Boston and New Haven. At the other end of the schedule spectrum, less-important trains making six intermediate stops trailed I-5s over the run in a still respectable three hours and 15 minutes. When the Shore Liners were in their pre-war prime, they handled 13 eastbound and 14 westbound trains every day. Eight I-5s could handle these trains in a rotation that kept two in reserve. The class even saw freight service in the aftermath of the devastating September 1938 hurricane, lifting 3,000 tons between New Haven and Boston with ease.

Binkerd's optimism aside, the New Haven was destined to be an early convert to diesel-electric power and the I-5s would prove to be the road's final steam purchase. They figured prominently in New Haven publicity and performed admirably on the demanding Shore Line route, but all were retired by early 1951.

A ZEPHYR BY ANY OTHER NAME

"The World's First Stainless Steel Streamline Steam Locomotive" was how the Burlington Route (Chicago, Burlington & Quincy) billed *Aeolus*, a Class S-4 Hudson given a shovel-nosed stainless steel shroud at the railroad's West Burlington, Iowa, shops and unveiled there in front of 5,000 onlookers on April 11, 1937. Such was the proliferation of streamlined steam that "firsts" were getting few and far between by the spring of 1937, but the publicity savvy Burlington—like the New Haven—was not one to pass up an opportunity.

The name *Aeolus*—the Keeper of the Winds in Greek mythology and pronounced "ee´-o-lus"—was Mrs. Goldie Murray's winning entry in a contest sponsored by the Burlington Junior Chamber of Commerce. The moniker actually was worn simultaneously for a time by two streamlined CB&Q Hudsons. No. 4000 (the former 3002) was followed by No. 4001, built new by the railroad at West Burlington in 1938. It did not take long for "Aeolus" to be corrupted into "Alice" by

"The World's First Stainless Steel Streamline Steam Locomotive," the Burlington Route's *Aeolus* No. 4000, on August 8, 1937—as events unfolded, a sheep in wolf's clothing. GRANT OAKES, JR.; J. M. GRUBER COLLECTION

THE ÆOLUS

The World's First STAINLESS STEEL STREAMLINE STEAM LOCOMOTIVE

This leaflet heralded *Aeolus'* April 1937 debut. AUTHOR'S COLLECTION

"Big Alice the Goon," No. 4000, with its middle Boxpok driver at Minneapolis in October 1938. A July 1939 view of No. 4001, also named *Aeolus*, shows slight variations in grill and skirt design. BOTH, HAROLD K. VOLLRATH COLLECTION

wags—as in "Big Alice the Goon," the unflattering nickname (borrowed from a character in the contemporary "Popeye" comic strip) by which No. 4000 was known to CB&Q railroaders for the rest of its career.

In describing the debut of No. 4000, the railroad stated, "This thrilling steam running mate for the Burlington's spectacular diesel-powered *Zephyrs* represents a definite program by the Burlington to ascertain the respective roles of steam and diesel power in the future of railroading."

Originally built in 1930 by Baldwin as one of an order for 14 Class S-4 Hudsons, No. 3002 spent the first seven years of its service life with its siblings leading heavy-weight CB&Q passenger trains on Chicago–Twin Cities and Chicago–Nebraska schedules. Moving consists that averaged 15 cars, the Hudsons earned high marks with Burlington management for their availability and low repair costs as compared to the Mountain- and heavy Pacific-types they replaced.

As built, the coal-burning S-4s rode on 78-inch drivers, employed 25x28-inch

cylinders, exerted a total 59,400 pounds of tractive force (including 11,700 pounds from a booster), weighed 207,730 pounds on drivers against a total engine weight of 391,880 pounds, and worked on 250 PSI of steam. Their 12-wheeled tenders held up to 24 tons of coal and 15,000 gallons of water.

While No. 4000's gleaming shroud caught the public's attention with its deliberate similarity to the road's trend-setting Budd-built *Zephyrs*, the real advance lay in the modifications made to its running gear during rebuilding.

A persistent curse of steam locomotives—and particularly of those intended for high-speed operation—was the need to precisely balance the heavy steel drive rods and other reciprocating parts in order to minimize the rhythmic pounding their weight and motion inflicted on the track structure and the locomotive itself. Toward this end, roller bearings and lighter-weight rods had become staples of the streamlined steam design engineers' repertoire.

During the rebuilding of No. 3002, the original piston rods, main pistons, crossheads, and main driving rods were replaced with components made from lightweight alloy steel. The new reciprocating parts weighed only 995 pounds per side, less than half of the originals. This reduced the locomotive's dynamic augment—the forces conspiring to "pound" the rails—to just one-third of the previous value at 100 MPH. Already equipped with roller bearings on its engine-truck and tender axles when it entered West Burlington for rebuilding, No. 3002 received the low-friction, low-maintenance bearings on its driver and trailer-truck axles as well as on all driving rods and valve-motion pins.

The weight savings achieved in the engine's reciprocating parts were offset by the addition of the stainless steel shrouding and its supporting framework. As with earlier fully-shrouded engines, the "new" No. 4000's running boards served as the foundation for the boiler, firebox, and smokebox shrouding. This removed the shroud panels from direct contact with these hot surfaces in order to prevent buckling. The skirts below the running board were clad in Budd fluting to match the *Zephyr* equipment, and hinged outward for maintenance access. Identical

fluting was carried back across the tender sides. Louvers flanking the awkwardly mounted headlight admitted air for smoke-lifting purposes.

Thanks to its retractable front coupler, No. 4000's nose was a broad expanse of stainless steel, originally adorned only with a rectangular red-and-black Burlington Route herald. All other engine and tender lettering was rendered in black. By September 1937, No. 4000's front end had been given a minor facelift. An anticlimber was installed for a measure of collision protection. Cosmetically, a pair of

Loewy-inspired "catwhiskers"—quintets of pinstripes curving forward from the edges of the nose and converging down to meet in a "V" at the new anticlimber—were added, as was a circular medallion depicting Aeolus. The Burlington Route herald had already been moved down and superimposed over the pinstripes.

The shroud applied to No. 4001—built at West Burlington in 1938—was virtually identical to its predecessor's, sharing No. 4000's later lettering and striping arrangement and with only slight changes to grill design and skirting.

Aeolus embodied a cost-effective alternative to new diesel-electric power, and was appraised on conventional CB&Q trains as well as serving as occasional backup power for the Chicago–Twin Cities *Twin Zephyrs* and the Chicago–Denver *Denver Zephyr*.

No. 4000 was photographed on February 26, 1938, as it prepared to lead the ten-car *Denver Zephyr* out of Denver Union Station and on the train's overnight trek to Chicago.
OTTO PERRY; DENVER PUBLIC LIBRARY WESTERN HISTORY COLLECTION

As for determining "the respective roles of steam and diesel power," on the Burlington, at least, there was no contest. The arrival of the first Electro-Motive E5s in 1940—a custom model for the CB&Q, clad in stainless steel fluting with noses styled to resemble their *Zephyr* powercar elders—signaled the end of *Aeolus'* relevance. No. 4000 lost its shroud in 1941, but remained "Big Alice the Goon" to crews until retired and preserved.

With Union Pacific 4-8-2 No. 7002 on the point, the *Forty-Niner* was near Cheyenne, Wyoming, on May 30, 1939. OTTO PERRY; DENVER PUBLIC LIBRARY WESTERN HISTORY COLLECTION

THE FORTY-NINER

The Burlington Route was not alone in developing streamlined steam for service on the High Plains in the spring of 1937.

The trio of railroads comprising the Chicago–San Francisco "Overland Route"—Southern Pacific, Union Pacific, and Chicago & North Western—had been experienced operators of diesel-powered long-distance streamliners since the launch of their jointly operated *City of Los Angeles* in 1936. UP's and C&NW's combined experience dated back to 1935 and the Chicago–Portland (Oregon) *City of Portland*.

On July 8, 1937, the three railroads inaugurated the extra-fare *Forty-Niner*, with a name celebrating both California's Gold Rush heritage and the train's 49-hour Oakland–Chicago eastbound schedule. Departing only five times per month from each of its end points, the train's schedule was arranged to offer every-third-day service in conjunction with the streamlined, diesel-powered *City of San Francisco*. The *Forty-Niner* was steam-powered throughout its run, with a custom consist of experimental lightweight and modernized heavyweight Pullmans.

The *Forty-Niner's* signature car was actually *two* cars—experimental articulated Pullmans *Bear Flag* and *California Republic*. The conjoined sleepers had been built by Pullman-Standard in 1935 and marked an evolutionary step away from fully articulated long-distance train-sets toward the eventuality of individual lightweight cars. *Bear Flag* was the former *Advance*, a 16 duplex single room sleeper renamed for *Forty-Niner* service. *California Republic* had been the *Progress*, a round-ended 3 bedroom, 1 compartment observation lounge similarly renamed for its stint on the new train. The pair weighed about as much as one older, conventional Pullman and rode on a pair of four-wheel trucks, with a six-wheel truck in the middle supporting the mated ends of both rib-roofed carbodies. Other members of the consist—all modernized Pullman heavyweights—were: *Gold Run*, *Captain John Sutter*, *Roaring Camp*, *Angels Camp*, and *Donner Lake*.

During the summers of 1939 and 1940, the *Forty-Niner*, the *City of San Francisco*, and the new *Treasure Island Special* (introduced on May 22, 1939) combined to provide every-second-day Overland Route departures in support of the west-coast World's Fair held on Treasure Island in San Francisco Bay. The *Treasure Island Special's* originally assigned observation car was even more noteworthy than the *Forty-Niner's*—none other than *George M. Pullman*, the 1933 hybrid recognized as the first lightweight passenger car. Re-equipped for its 1940 season, the *Treasure Island Special's* markers were carried by yet another Pullman celebrity, 2 bedroom, 1 compartment, 1 drawing room observation lounge *American Milemaster*, itself an exhibit at the 1939 New York World's Fair.

On Union Pacific's portion of the Overland Route, heavy Pacific No. 2906 led the *Forty-Niner* between Omaha and Cheyenne, where similarly shrouded 4-8-2 No. 7002 took over in deference to the grades of Sherman Hill before handing the train over to the Southern Pacific at Ogden, Utah.

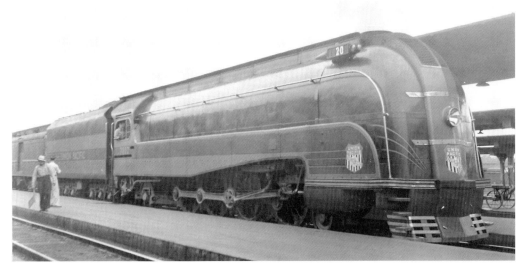

No. 7002 was at Denver Union Station in August 1940. The chrome-bedecked nose contours and slatted pilots of UP's two streamlined steam locomotives bore more than a passing resemblance to the Electro-Motive unit that led the 1936 *City of Denver* across the Overland Route.
HAROLD K. VOLLRATH COLLECTION

Pacific No. 2906 had been built by Baldwin in 1920, and Mountain No. 7002 was an Alco alumnus of 1922. Both were coal-fired. Modernized in 1936 to serve as backup power for the growing fleet of diesel-powered *City* streamliners, the two locomotives were equipped with roller bearings and lightweight Timken rods, Boxpok drivers, paired Sellers injectors, larger exhaust stacks, and improved brake equipment, among other refinements.

No. 2906 weighed 193,450 pounds on drivers against a total engine weight of 308,700 pounds; the respective weights for the larger No. 7002 were 257,500 and 382,500 pounds. The Pacific could produce 42,500 pounds of tractive force; the Mountain, 54,838 pounds.

Their recent upgrading and prior service on the Overland Route made the pair obvious candidates when UP Vice-President William Jeffers and Otto Jablemann opted to streamline two steam locomotives for the new *Forty-Niner*. Both locomotives received bulb-nosed streamlined shrouding in April 1937, designed by UP mechanical officer Wayne Owens and installed at the road's Omaha shops.

Two horizontal channels flanked and largely concealed a narrow skyline casing

Union Pacific No. 7002 led a heavyweight *Challenger* consist on its Overland Route passage in this circa 1938 view.
TLC PUBLISHING COLLECTION

Union Pacific's other streamlined steam locomotive was Pacific No. 2902, photographed at Denver Union Station in June 1940.
HAROLD K. VOLLRATH COLLECTION

atop both locomotives' boilers. Running board skirting was cut away on No. 2906 to reveal the Pacific's 77-inch drivers, while this skirting on No. 7002 swept down to partially conceal all but the frontmost of the Mountain's 73-inch driving wheels. The influence of Otto Kuhler's published conceptual drawings was apparent in the UP engines' new cab windows, with their multi-paned glazing set within an oval frame.

The shrouding of No. 2906 extended to the Pacific's Vanderbilt tender, which had its 12,000-gallon cylindrical cistern enclosed to match the flat-sided styling of No. 7002. Beyond some rooftop fairings, no attempt was made to enclose the rear of the locomotives' cabs or hide the gangway opening between engine and tender.

The shrouds' nose contours and low-mounted headlight were reminiscent of Dreyfuss' work on NYC's *Mercury*, but there the similarity ended. Where the *Mercury* locomotive's shroud wore a subdued gray, Union Pacific gave its streamlined twins a striking livery of Leaf Brown and the road's recently adopted Armour Yellow, with red striping. The pilot, nose, boiler, running gear, and cab and tender tops of both locomotives were brown. Yellow was used in a vertical band up the center of the nose, and along the running board skirts and the sides of the cab and tender. Stylized red wings on the cylinder skirting flowed back in a wide band across the cab and tender. A trio of pinstripes—evoking the "catwhiskers" used by Raymond Loewy in his 1935 restyling of the PRR GG-1—flowed up and back from the pilot beam and disappeared into the running board steps. Bands of chrome trim

were applied to the pilot and nose, and the louvered air intake at the top of the nose was also rendered in chrome.

The two were the first UP locomotives to wear the road's new sans-serif style of lettering, introduced the previous month.

Both locomotives contrasted with the *Forty-Niner* cars' special Pullman scheme of metallic bronze-gray (gunmetal) with black roofs and gold-and-black striping.

The *Forty-Niner* was discontinued on July 27, 1941, and its place in the Overland Route streamliner rotation taken by an additional, newly delivered *City of San Francisco* consist with diesels at the helm.

The *Forty-Niner* consist was disbanded, and the cars repainted into Pullman's then-standard two-tone gray "pool" colors. The pair of streamlined UP locomotives lost their shrouds but continued to pull passenger trains on the Overland Route and elsewhere.

THE NEW ROYAL BLUE

Otto Kuhler took his interest in bullet-nosed streamlined steam beyond the drawing board with a boldly won commission to create an all-new *Royal Blue* for the Baltimore & Ohio in 1937. Critical of the 1935 edition of the train and the English lines of its locomotive, Kuhler came away from a meeting with B&O President Daniel Willard with a new client and a new challenge.

Retained as the B&O's Consulting Engineer of Design, Kuhler was given responsibility for the interior layout and decoration of a new eight-car *Royal Blue* consist. The railroad's Mount Clare shops created the train by modernizing a group of obsolete heavyweight cars. In a transformation similar to that crafted by Henry Dreyfuss for NYC's 1936 *Mercury*, Mount Clare retained the heavyweight cars' basic architecture but added arched roofs, full-width diaphragms, folding steps, and deep underbody skirts for a cost-effective streamstyled look.

Kuhler's modernized consist replaced the superficially similar 1935 AC&F trainset that had been reassigned from the *Royal Blue's* Washington, DC–Jersey City route to B&O's Alton subsidiary in Illinois (see Chapter 2). Concerns over the AC&F cars' riding qualities had influenced the decision to rebuild heavyweights cars for the new consist.

The 1937 *Royal Blue* comprised a baggage-smoker, three coaches, a lunch counter-coach, a diner, a parlor car, and a blunt-ended lounge-observation car. Collectively, the cars could accommodate 272 revenue passengers—eight fewer than the 1935 *Royal Blue*—and also offered 14 lunch counter seats, 44 places in the diner, and 42 non-revenue seats in the observation car.

Taking cues from Dreyfuss' New York Central *Mercury*, Kuhler styled his *Royal Blue* as a flow-through unit, varying the use of a core color palette to give each car's interior an individual look within a consistent overall scheme. Like Dreyfuss, Kuhler recognized the importance of lighting, both as a practical necessity and an effective design element.

The exterior of the new train was given a stately livery of blue, gray, and black with gold lettering and striping, accented by cast B&O Capitol Dome monograms.

Adorning the rear of the observation car was a traditional lighted drumhead sign bearing the train's name. In one form or another, Kuhler's blue and gray would remain the B&O's passenger equipment colors for more than three decades.

Kuhler's *Royal Blue* commission extended to the design of a streamlined steam locomotive for the train. Ten-year-old Class P-7 Pacific No. 5304, delivered as *President Monroe*, became the first steam locomotive to receive what became the designer's trademark bullet nose. The 4-6-2 was one of 20 built by Baldwin in 1927 as Nos. 5300-5319. Painted olive green and named after the first 21 U.S. presidents (*President Adams*, No. 5301, honored both chief executives of that name), B&O's "President Class" was assigned to passenger service between metropolitan New York and the nation's capital. Blue paint later replaced these locomotives' original green livery.

With B&O Pacific No. 5304, Otto Kuhler finally was able to see his passion for streamlining that retained "the characteristic features of the steam locomotive" come to fruition. B&O PHOTO; AUTHOR'S COLLECTION

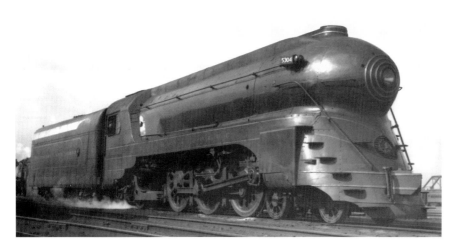

B&O No. 5304 was in full stride with the eight-car, modernized heavyweight *Royal Blue* at Ewing, New Jersey, in November 1937.

Kuhler's *Royal Blue* Pacific was photographed at the Communipaw, N. J., engine terminal in July 1937.
BOTH, HAROLD K. VOLLRATH COLLECTION

No. 5304's shrouding generally resembled that applied by Raymond Loewy to Pennsylvania Railroad K-4s No. 3768 the year before, with the locomotive's major elements—boiler, smokebox, pilot, cab—smoothed yet readily discernable. Such retention of the locomotive's "basic form" had been one of Kuhler's most frequently repeated conceptual themes, and would form the basis of most of his steam locomotive styling commissions.

No. 5304's transformation went beyond mere cosmetics, however. The Pacific's original 27x28-inch cylinders were rebored (to 27.5 inches), its 14-inch piston valves replaced with 12-inch double-admission valves, and its boiler pressure raised from 230 PSI to 240 PSI. Combined with new Boxpok drivers retaining the original 80-inch diameter, these changes raised No. 5304's tractive

effort from 50,000 pounds to 54,000 pounds. Along with other modifications—most notably the installation of lighter rods and a B&O-designed semi-watertube firebox— No. 5304's rebuilding was thorough enough to warrant moving the engine into its very own P-7a class.

Although a vestibule-type cab was applied at rebuilding, the gap between engine and tender was not bridged by the gasket or curtain arrangements used on other recent streamlinings.

Stretching the original tender by 4.5 feet increased its water tank size from 11,000 to 13,000 gallons, and permitted 19.5 tons of coal to be carried vs. the original bunker's 17.5-ton capacity. The tender's roofline matched the height of the trailing cars, although coal was often heaped above this silhouette.

A trio of concentric chrome rings surrounded the locomotive's headlight, and chrome strips accented the pilot. The train's name was applied to the engine's running board skirts in gold paint, with like-colored striping sweeping back from a cast B&O Capitol Dome monogram mounted above the pilot. A similar casting was placed forward on each side of the tender, ahead of the railroad's name. This tender decoration was enclosed in gold striping that made a curious upward jog in order to match the windowband striping of the cars—placing the tender stripes at a more appropriate height would have located them in line with two unfortunately positioned rows of rivets.

No. 5304 made its debut on the new *Royal Blue* on December 9, 1937, three months after Kuhler's modernized cars had entered service. Although the locomotive lost its streamlining in 1939—after Electro-Motive E-units had bumped it from the *Royal Blue*—its days in the limelight were not over. After soldiering through the war as just another B&O Pacific, No. 5304 was destined to become the second of two American steam locomotives to be *re*streamlined. The engine's swan song on B&O's *Cincinnatian* is described in Chapter 4.

"CLAD IN SHINING ARMOR"

The Reading Railroad made headlines with the December 13, 1937, introduction of an innovative five-car stainless steel streamliner made bidirectional by virtue of having a pug-ended observation car on each end. The initial expense of the second observation car was more than offset by the savings in not having to turn the train at its congested Philadelphia and Jersey City (N.J.) end terminals. Although not the first stainless steel train in the East—that honor had gone in 1935 to the Boston & Maine–Maine Central *Flying Yankee*, a near twin of Burlington's original *Zephyr*—the Reading consist did qualify as the East's first non-articulated, locomotive-hauled stainless steel train. Its schedule called for two daily round trips over the 90.3-mile route.

Following a train-naming contest that awarded a $250 prize to P. W. Silzer for his winning entry, the new train was christened the *Crusader* by opera star Lily Pons at a February 23, 1938, ceremony.

With a tavern-diner at its center, the single *Crusader* consist, as built, also included two full coaches between the pair of coach-observation cars.

Architect Paul Cret, with close ties to Philadelphia's Budd Company, was largely responsible for the striking exterior appearance of the builder's stainless steel passenger cars, and his hand was also seen in the pair of steam locomotives streamlined to pull the *Crusader*.

A pair of Class G-1sa Pacifics, built in 1918, was sent to the road's Reading (Pa.) shops to receive shovel-nosed shrouds that made extensive use of stainless steel in sheet and fluted form. The rationale behind Reading's choice of steam power for its new state-of-the-art train lay in the company being an "anthracite road" with strong economic and political ties to the coal industry.

Pacifics Nos. 117 and 118 emerged from the shops with their 80-inch spoked drivers intact, but otherwise belied their age. They tipped the scales at 273,600 pounds each before rebuilding; shrouding and related modifications added 32,740 pounds to engine and tender.

A broad band of stainless steel extended up the nose and around the headlight before curving back onto the to of the shroud in front of the stack. It was flanked at the rounded top of the nose by a pair of stainless steel air intake grills. A broad skirting panel angled up from each side of the smooth pilot and pilot beam to the height of the cars' letterboards. The

Reading's five-car *Crusader* employed observation cars at each end to save the time and expense of turning cars at Jersey City and Philadelphia, the train's congested end terminals. The *Crusader* was the first locomotive-hauled stainless steel train in the East. BUDD COMPANY PHOTO; AUTHOR'S COLLECTION

As power for its new *Crusader*, Reading rebuilt two veteran Pacifics and shrouded them in blue-trimmed stainless steel, complete with Budd Company fluting to match the cars. The aft portion of the tender sides were extended rearward to envelop the rounded end of the observation car. J. R. QUINN COLLECTION

The *Crusader* paused under wire during a pre-inaugural run. READING PHOTO; AUTHOR'S COLLECTION

decorative treatment of this stainless steel skirt matched the alternately flat and fluted nature of the Budd cars' architecture. Those areas of the shroud covering the nose and boiler which were not stainless steel were painted a strong blue.

Following the train's February 1938 official christening, the CRUSADER name was applied, in ornate blue lettering, to a stainless panel mounted on the forward portion of the skirt, and also on a nameplate on each side of the dining car.

The shrouding and train name provided a splash of color before blending engine and tender almost seamlessly into the trailing consist. The impression of continuity was enhanced by a seven-foot extension of the roof and sides at the rear of the tender—this closed the gap ahead of the pug end of the leading observation car while still allowing necessary operational clearances.

The streamlined Pacifics rolled out of the Reading shops as Class G-1sa's in November 1937. On the 29th of that month, the new train made its first public appearance on a press run between Philadelphia and Hershey, Pennsylvania.

The new train was operated in conjunction with the Jersey Central, over whose track it ran for the 30-some miles between Jersey City and Bound Brook, New Jersey. From that point to Philadelphia, the *Crusader* was on home rails. Schedules were arranged to suit Philadelphia-based financial types desiring to reach Wall Street before the morning bell, and return them home after a busy day's trading. In between, the consist made a second daily trip to Philadelphia and back. Typical timing for the run was about 1.5 hours. Manhattan-bound shoppers and matinee-hounds could ride the *Crusader's* similar Saturday rotation, but the train was sidelined for maintenance every Sunday.

Although Reading and Jersey Central competed with "Royal Blue Line" partner B&O for Philadelphia–New York traffic, all three railroads had the mighty Pennsy in their crosshairs on this route. Describing "a distinguished train between Philadelphia and New York," Reading's advertising for its new train suggestively sniped at the Pennsy's outdated, non-air-conditioned coaches: "... the *Crusader* combines every modern facility for complete travel ease and relaxation, with a charm and beauty

Stainless Steel Streamlined Train

PHILADELPHIA and NEW YORK

Reading-Jersey Central

EFFECTIVE MAY 23, 1943

PHILADELPHIA TRAINS

AIR-CONDITIONED EQUIPMENT
Cars for thru passengers on trains between New York and Philadelphia are completely air-conditioned.

Streamlined TRAIN

Crusader
IT OF SHINING ARMOR

LUXURIOUS COMFORT WITH ECONOMY

TIME TABLES
BETWEEN
NEW YORK
AND
PHILADELPHIA

TT100 (62A)   5-17-43   10M   Order No. 18483

AUTHOR'S COLLECTION

of interior decoration that will amaze— and delight—those accustomed to the drab monotony of the trains of yesterday."

Reading enjoyed double-digit ridership increases on the Philadelphia–Jersey City route following the *Crusader's* debut, and the train developed a loyal passenger following. The streamlined Pacifics lasted in their intended service until 1948, when they were replaced by new 4-6-2s and reassigned. These vaguely Anglicized, homebuilt Pacifics only lasted on the *Crusader* until 1950, when they in turn were replaced—this time by diesels in the form of EMD FP7A's.

The two Pacifics streamlined for the *Crusader's* debut were retired and scrapped in 1952. The cars fared better, lasting in Reading service until they were sold as a set to Canadian National in 1964. Refurbished and renamed *Le Champlain*, they were not retired until the early 1980s.

Santa Fe's "Blue Goose"—streamlined Baldwin Hudson No. 3460—was center stage at this 1938 Chicago gathering of the road's new passenger train fleet. The Hudson's two-tone blue livery made it an odd duck at this lineup—all of the freshly Simonized E1s were dressed in Leland Knickerbocker's memorable red-and-yellow "Warbonnet" scheme. ELECTRO-MOTIVE PHOTO; AUTHOR'S COLLECTION

THE BLUE GOOSE

When the Atchison, Topeka & Santa Fe (AT&SF) contracted with Baldwin in November 1936 to build six Hudsons and 11 Northerns (4-8-4) for fast passenger service, the road opted to have one of each class streamlined for assignment to portions of the forthcoming lightweight *Chief's* flagship Chicago–Los Angeles schedule.

While weight restrictions forced railroad and builder to abandon streamlining of the burly 4-8-4, Hudson No. 3460 was customized to become Santa Fe's only streamlined steam locomotive.

The 17 passenger locomotives were designed under the direction of Santa Fe Mechanical Engineer H. H. Lanning, with No. 3460 given a torpedo-nosed skyline shroud that incurred a $15,000 premium over its five unstreamlined classmates.

The new 3460-class Hudsons were intended to augment and improve upon a group of earlier Santa Fe 4-6-4s. Acquired as replacements for outmoded Pacifics, Nos. 3450-3459 dated to 1927 and had

A Baldwin builder's view of Santa Fe No. 3460. AUTHOR'S COLLECTION

undergone individual and collective modifications over the years.

The Santa Fe's new Hudsons were brutes, overshadowing their predecessors by any standard of measurement. Drivers measuring 84 inches across conveyed the engines' 49,300 pounds of tractive force. Boiler pressure was 300 PSI. The streamlined No. 3460's weight on drivers of 211,400 pounds was slightly less than the 213,440 pounds of Nos. 3461-3465, but the shroud added roughly 8,000 pounds of dead weight not carried by the others.

Roller bearings were employed on all engine and tender axles. All were oil-fired, although provision was made in the tenders for later conversion to stoker-fed coal. No. 3460's tender carried 7,107 gallons of fuel oil and 20,000 gallons of water. In comparison, the others toted 7,000 gallons and 21,000 gallons, respectively.

Although Nos. 3461-3465 arrived from Baldwin in October and November 1937, streamlined No. 3460 was not delivered until January 1938—still in time for the February debut of the new *Chief*, though.

Road-weary—note the crumpled pilot sheeting—but still sporting full skirting over the cylinders and under the cab, Santa Fe's "Blue Goose" worked a heavyweight consist in this prewar view.
JOE SCHMITZ COLLECTION

The streamlining applied to No. 3460 superficially resembled the New Haven Shore Liners—not surprising, perhaps, given the timing and location of the Santa Fe engines' construction. A not-quite-hemispherical nose flowed back into the sheathed boiler, with the whole affair capped by a full-length skyline casing. A basket-like grill above the nose, flanked by teardrop-shaped marker lights, admitted air for smoke-lifting. A boxy fairing bridged the gap between nosecone and smooth pilot, and deep skirting covered the cylinders. This tapered into a running board skirt that cleared the drivers and trailing truck before curving down below the cab to the level of the tender side sill. Coved metal fairings suggested the presence of a coal bunker in the tender, but were merely a device to blend the considerable height of the engine into the trailing cars' roofline.

The engine's two-tone blue paint gave rise almost immediately to the nickname "Blue Goose." Running gear was painted a deep bluish gray, with tires edged in aluminum paint. An 18-inch-deep strip of stainless steel ran along the upper portion of the running board skirt and continued across the tender at the same height, and narrowed slightly to flow down to and across the pilot. (As early as 1939, all skirting below the stainless band had been removed, except for a vestige under the cab.) Three still-narrower stainless strips divided the pilot, and an oval SANTA FE monogram was placed on the flat fairing

below the nosecone. Etched into the wide stainless steel band were the road number (above the drivers) and the road name (on the tender). The road number also appeared, for a short time after delivery, painted on each side of the tender below the stainless trim.

Following public displays in Los Angeles and Chicago—where the "Blue Goose" rubbed shoulders with brand-new Electro-Motive E1s in their stunning Warbonnet livery—No. 3460 entered full-time revenue service alongside the other five new Hudsons between Chicago and La Junta, Colorado. The engines routinely made this 991.7-mile trip without change, and managed to hold the diesels at bay by virtue of their high availability and low maintenance costs. The Santa Fe's streamlined tide was running Warbonnet red, however, and the 3460-class found themselves bumped to lesser routes after yeoman's service during the war. They migrated to shorter runs in Kansas, Oklahoma, New Mexico, and Texas.

No. 3460 retained its streamlining to the end, with minor skirting modifications. The "Blue Goose" bowed out as a celebrity, with its February 27, 1954, final run made during filming of a company promotional film at Kansas City's Argentine Yard. The engine's role? It was cast as one of five singularly significant locomotives—three steam, two diesel—in the Santa Fe's evolution to a modern, dieselized property. Fame, however, did not save it from the scrapper.

By the time of this February 1948 view at Chillicothe, Illinois, No. 3460 had lost its cylinder skirts and most of the under-cab skirting. Note the stack extension.
HAROLD K. VOLLRATH COLLECTION

NORTH WESTERN'S GREEN GIANTS

As "dropper of the gauntlet" among the three railroads ultimately competing for the high-speed Chicago–Twin Cities passenger trade, the Chicago & North Western (C&NW) nonetheless lagged behind the Burlington Route and the Milwaukee Road in offering the latest motive power and equipment on the route. With its competitors' streamlined *Twin Zephyrs* and *Hiawathas* well established and well patronized, the C&NW waited until September 24, 1939, to unveil the first of its dieselized, streamlined "*400*" speedsters.

The C&NW had taken the first step toward a streamlined future 18 months earlier, however, when it placed the first of nine shrouded Hudsons in service between Chicago and Omaha. This was the C&NW's 488-mile stretch of the joint (with UP and SP) Overland Route, and the new Class E-4 locomotives were entrusted with the route's premier limiteds. They were, at any rate, too heavy to have served on the Twin Cities "*400*" route.

Nos. 4001-4009 were built by Alco and delivered during March and April 1938. There was a hint of "Hiawatha" in the E-4s' shovel-nosed streamlining, influenced at some level, perhaps, by the Milwaukee Road's Otto Kuhler-styled Hudsons then under development at the same builder.

North Western promoted its new power in a 1938 brochure as "The Steamliners" and "the most powerful 4-6-4 passenger locomotives ever built." Hyperbole, seemingly never far from a streamlined steamer, was no stranger to the C&NW's public relations department: "The nine streamlined locomotives now in service on the Chicago & North Western Railway are the newest and finest 'Iron Horses' used in passenger transportation. They are thoroughbreds in every respect. With their sleek green and gold jackets of lightweight steel, they embody the latest in streamline design; combining utility with beauty of line.

"These new modern 'Steamliners' with their huge 84-inch disc wheel[s] and 55,000 pounds of tractive power can generate 5,000 horsepower at 70 miles per hour. They are capable of speeds up to 120 miles per hour and can haul a 15-car passenger train with ease at 80 miles per hour."

They *were* big, with an engine weight of 412,000 pounds. Of that, 216,000

pounds was borne by the drivers. Steam pressure was 300 PSI; cylinder dimensions 25x29 inches. Tenders carried 25 tons of coal and 20,000 gallons of water, and their capacity meant that three replenishing stops required by older power between Chicago and Omaha could be dropped.

The Boxpok drivers' axles were equipped with roller bearings, as were the engine truck, trailing truck, and tender axles. Timken and SKF divided the spoils.

The steel shroud incorporated a full-length skyline casing. Wide skirts left most of the running gear exposed in a bow to maintenance access. The nose was capped by what had become the usual grilled air intake but boasted not one, but two headlights. The North Western was a pioneer in the use of oscillating warning lights on its locomotives, and an early model produced by the Mars Signal Light Company was housed above the regular headlight.

The Chicago & North Western's E-4 streamlined Hudsons were delivered with a conventional headlight and, above it, an oscillating warning light. The railroad later added a larger warning light, and moved the fixed-beam headlight to a lower position on the nose.
C&NW PHOTO; AUTHOR'S COLLECTION

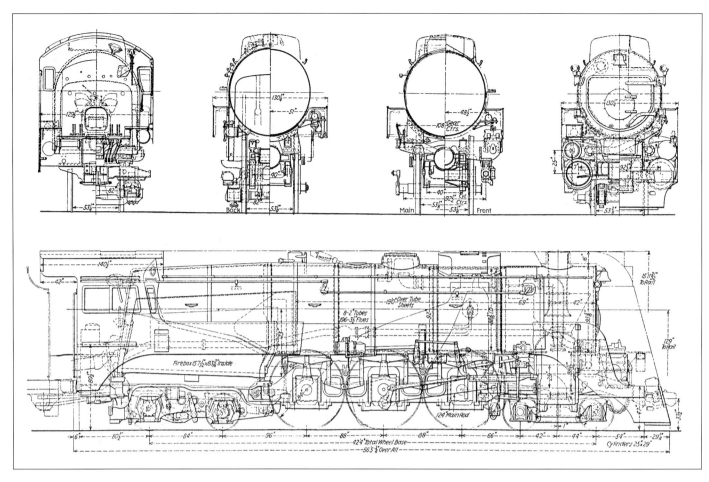

Cross sections and side elevation of a C&NW E-4 Hudson, showing the relationship of the shrouding with the locomotive underneath.
RAILWAY MECHANICAL ENGINEER

Access to the smokebox and other front-end components was afforded by clamshell doors, a common arrangement on shovel-nosed locomotives. C&NW PHOTO; AUTHOR'S COLLECTION

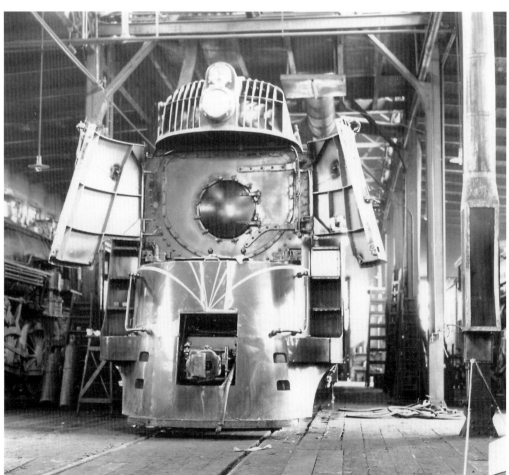

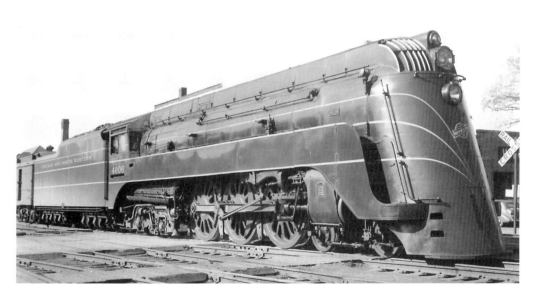

C&NW E-4 No. 4003 as delivered in early 1938. Engine and tender were dark green with gold striping. C&NW PHOTO; AUTHOR'S COLLECTION

No. 4006, at Cedar Rapids, Iowa, in March 1940, reveals modifications made to the E-4 Hudsons after they entered service. Most apparent are the revised headlight configuration and the addition of louvers to the coupler compartment door. HAROLD K. VOLLRATH COLLECTION

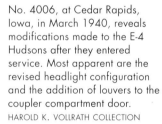

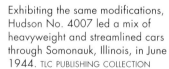

Exhibiting the same modifications, Hudson No. 4007 led a mix of heavyweight and streamlined cars through Somonauk, Illinois, in June 1944. TLC PUBLISHING COLLECTION

Smooth Flowing Speed
THE STEAMLINERS
MOST POWERFUL 4-6-4 PASSENGER LOCOMOTIVES EVER BUILT
Chicago & North Western Ry.

The engine and tender were painted Pullman green, relieved only by a small C&NW herald on the upper nose, gold lettering, and three gold stripes that met in a "V" above the pilot.

Eight Overland Route trains—among them the *Forty-Niner*, the *Pacific Limited*, the *Challengers*, and the *Los Angeles Lim-ited*—routinely were assigned one of the new E-4s, with the ninth locomotive held as protection power. Consists of these predominantly heavyweight trains ranged from eight to 18 cars. Demoted by diesels after the war and assigned to less-prestigious duties, the last of the E-4s had left the C&NW roster by late 1953.

The C&NW touted its new "Steamliners" in this 1938 leaflet. AUTHOR'S COLLECTION

ABOVE RIGHT: Brand-new E-4 No. 4001 led Train No. 49, the westbound *Forty-Niner*, through Austin station and out of Chicago on March 14, 1938. A. W. JOHNSON

No. 4009 sped the *Pacific Limited*, Train No. 21, west through Maywood, Illinois, on December 18, 1938. A. W. JOHNSON

THE DREYFUSS HUDSONS

The 4-6-4 wheel arrangement's most common nickname was a legacy of the New York Central's status as the first railroad to place one in service (in February 1927).

NYC was famed for its "Water Level Route" between New York and Chicago—a not-so-subtle dig at rival Pennsy's more arduous route through, not around, the Alleghenies. The Hudson and Mohawk Rivers figured prominently in NYC's easy profile, so when a name was sought for the new 4-6-4, "Hudson" it was. The road created a couple more fluvial names for its steam classes: "Mountain" and "Northern" wouldn't do for an essentially gradeless Eastern route, so 4-8-2s were Mohawks on the New York Central, and 4-8-4s were known as Niagaras.

The ten Hudsons styled by Henry Dreyfuss to lead the *20th Century Limited* and other celebrated members of New York Central's "Great Steel Fleet" are the enduring icons of the prewar streamline era on America's railroads.

Their number was rounded to a baker's dozen with inclusion of the restreamlined No. 5344—the erstwhile *Commodore Vanderbilt*—in 1939, and a dissimilar but arguably even more striking treatment of Nos. 5426 and 5429 for the *Empire State Express* in 1941.

NYC Nos. 5445-5454 were the last ten of an order for 50 Class J-3a Hudsons built by Alco. The 40 nonstreamlined locomotives were delivered in late 1937, and the shrouded examples followed in March and April 1938, just in time to lead the Great Steel Fleet's streamlined showdown with Pennsy's "Fleet of Modernism."

Collectively, these 50 NYC "Super Hudsons" incorporated a wide range of power and performance improvements over their older Class J-1 stablemates. Drawbar horsepower, for instance, was 3,880 at 65 MPH, 21% greater than the J-1. J-3a boiler pressure was 275 PSI vs. 225 on the J-1, and the capacity of the new engines' boilers was roughly 10% greater than their predecessors.

Half of the J-3a Hudsons had 79-inch Scullin disc drivers, with Boxpok wheels applied to the other 25—this 50:50 split

Just delivered, the first three of New York Central's streamlined Hudsons—Nos. 5445, 5446, and 5447—lined up at Rensselaer, N.Y., in March 1938. NYC PHOTO; NYCSHS COLLECTION

Designer Henry Dreyfuss' final exterior rendering for the 1938 *20th Century Limited*. NYC PHOTO; NYCSHS COLLECTION

For locomotives widely regarded as icons of streamlined form, the NYC Hudsons had plenty of protruding piping and machinery. Brand-new No. 5445 was photographed in March 1938. NYC PHOTO; NYCSHS COLLECTION

Henry Dreyfuss created a classic Art Deco design with his 1935 Thermos carafe and tray. Did the handle and body foreshadow his equally famous J-3a nose styling?

also was demonstrated on the streamlined engines. The total engine weight of a non-streamlined J-3a was 360,000 pounds; Dreyfuss' streamlining added a modest 5,500 pounds to this figure. Weight on drivers was 196,000 pounds, about three percent more than a J-1. All axles were fitted with roller bearings: Timken units on the engine and SKF on the tender. Five of the streamlined J-3a's had Timken roller bearings fitted to their drive rods, as well.

As delivered, a J-3a tender could carry 30 tons of coal and 14,000 gallons of water. Equipped with air-operated water scoops, they could replenish their tanks on the run from NYC's extensive network of mainline track pans.

In his "less-is-more" streamlining of the ten J-3a locomotives, Dreyfuss abandoned the earlier "bathtub" shroud of his *Mercury* in favor of a form-fitting, torpedo-nosed skin. Faithful to early renderings, a smooth pilot and front-end skirt were topped by a hemispherical nose. A full-length skyline casing concealed stack and domes, although vestiges of the countersunk Elesco feedwater heater were left visible above the smokebox. Side skirting was limited to a sloping panel below the cab, curving upward and extending only as far forward as the middle driver. The engine's running gear and cylinders were thus entirely exposed, as was the forward half of the running board and its steps. The signature element of the

The final five streamlined J-3a Hudsons were fitted with Scullin's distinctive disc drivers. Dreyfuss highlighted the drivers on all ten streamlined Hudsons—the other five rolled on more conventional Boxpoks—by calling for them to be painted aluminum. NYC PHOTOS; NYCSHS COLLECTION

streamlining was an aluminum crest that deepened as it arched up the front of the nose. Its flow broken only by the slightly below-center headlight, the crest merged into the skyline casing ahead of the stack, where it divided a backswept smoke-lifting air intake.

The appearance of this crest has often been likened to the helmets worn by Spartan warriors in ancient times, but it actually bore a striking resemblance to one of Dreyfuss' earlier design commissions. If tipped on its side, the spout and handle of his 1935 Thermos™ carafe—an Art Deco

classic—hinted at the much larger "hot water bottles" to come.

Aluminum was employed in the construction of the cab, running boards, and dome casing. Underbody skirting and a raised roofline helped the tenders blend with the lightweight Pullman-Standard cars the Hudsons were intended to pull. Overall medium gray paint was accented by a dark gray band on the tender sides, with aluminum and blue striping, that matched the trailing cars' windowband treatment. Running gear was also painted a darker shade of gray. The headlight case, cylinder head covers, and handrails were left in unpainted aluminum, and a cast New York Central oval medallion, with raised lettering on a blue background, was mounted above the pilot. Drivers and nose fin were painted aluminum, to particularly striking effect on the quintet of streamlined Hudsons (Nos. 5450-5454) equipped with Scullin disc wheels. Lettering was done in aluminum paint.

The ten streamlined J-3a's were most closely associated with the 1938 edition of New York Central's flagship *20th Century Limited.* This was the first lightweight, streamlined incarnation of the celebrated New York–Chicago train, which traced its pedigree back to 1902 and the promotionally fertile mind of NYC's General Passenger Agent, George H. Daniels.

The train's 1938 edition was launched with much fanfare on June 15—the same day that rival Pennsylvania's newly streamlined *Broadway Limited* made its debut between the same two cities. The two trains had much in common. NYC and Pennsy—arch rivals to the core—nonetheless cooperated with the Pullman Company and its Pullman-Standard car-building division to minimize the expense of duplicated effort and one-upmanship. The cooperation meant that Pullman was not put in a position of playing favorites with its two biggest customers, and for the railroads it was a means of keeping their supplier "honest." Both trains, although far from identical, therefore shared much in the way of the latest accommodations and equipment design. They differed most apparently in their exterior liveries and the division and decor of their public spaces, both of which reflected another high-profile rivalry.

Raymond Loewy gave the Pennsy streamliners of 1938—the "Fleet of Modernism"—a rich Tuscan red and maroon exterior accented with gold pinstripes, and his interiors were colorful and inviting. Dreyfuss' *Century* was more subdued and refined, as was his style, making extensive use inside and out of grays, blues, and bare metals—prompting the never-shy Loewy to publicly wonder whether his professional colleague was color-blind.

New York Central greeted the streamlined era with 52 Pullman-Standard lounge and all-room sleeping cars, six diners, a quartet of postal-baggage cars, and an unprecedented 16-hour New York–Chicago overnight schedule. All cars had smooth, welded sides and skirted underbodies. Full-width diaphragms gave the train an unbroken appearance, and tight-lock couplers ensured a smooth ride. Sleeping accommodations were divided among five floor plans: the 17-roomette (with a porter's section) *City* series; 10-roomette, 5-double bedroom *Cascade* series; 4-bedroom, 4-compartment, 2-drawing room *Imperial* series; 13-bedroom *County* series; and the 1-drawing room, 1-bedroom *Island* series. The *Century's* feature cars were the four *Island*-series sleeper-lounge-observations, each equipped to carry the train's signature blue-lighted tail sign on their sleek rounded ends.

A steady flow of additional lightweight equipment from P-S—and, to a lesser extent, Budd—between 1938 and 1940 permitted more members of the steam-powered Great Steel Fleet to be streamlined. The Dreyfuss J-3a's could be seen at the helm of various fleet members—trains like the *Commodore Vanderbilt*, *Ohio State Limited*, *Empire State Express*, and *Upstate Special*—sharing duties with non-streamlined Hudsons, Mohawks, and, after the war, Niagaras.

The jutting profile of Dreyfuss' Hudsons was immediately linked not only with the *20th Century Limited* but with the entire railroad, and for a time appeared in advertisements, timetables, menus, and elsewhere as an integral adjunct to the company's oval monogram.

Modifications to the streamlined J-3a's over the years saw the forward portion of the already abbreviated running board skirt removed circa 1941. At least one, No. 5446, is known to have operated without its rounded smokebox cover in September

Under the gaze of Ceres, high atop the Board of Trade Building, a streamlined Hudson leads the *20th Century Limited* through the throat of La Salle Street Station and into its overnight trip to New York in August 1938. NYC PHOTO; NYCSHS COLLECTION

1941. Long-distance "PT" tenders—dubbed "Centipedes" for their 14-wheel undercarriages—were mated to the streamlined Hudsons beginning in mid-1943. This change eliminated the need for coaling stops between Harmon, N.Y., (where steam swapped consists with electric power to and from Manhattan's Grand Central Terminal) and Buffalo.

In July 1939 No. 5344, famous since 1934 as the shrouded *Commodore Vanderbilt*, was restreamlined to match the ten Dreyfuss Hudsons. Unnamed, the dark gray locomotive was assigned to the new *Chicago Mercury* service upon that train's November 12, 1939, debut, along with No. 5445. The erstwhile *Commodore Vanderbilt* ran in this guise for almost six years before being unstreamlined in the aftermath of an October 1945 grade-crossing collision in East Chicago.

One streamlined Hudson met an even more cataclysmic fate in September 1943, when J-3a No. 5450 suffered a boiler explosion near Canastota, New York. Three crewmembers were killed, but the engine was rebuilt after a 13-month hiatus and returned to service.

Another 1939 addition to NYC's Chicago–New York parade was the *Pacemaker*, an all-coach train composed of modernized heavyweight cars and launched to meet the competition of the Pennsy's similarly equipped *Trail Blazer*.

With lightning-striped NYC diesels making steady inroads in the postwar Great Steel Fleet, beginning with E7s assigned to the *20th Century Limited* in 1945, the Dreyfuss Hudsons were bumped from their "prestige runs." Shorn of their streamlining in 1946 and 1947, all were retired by early 1956 and scrapped.

A pre-inaugural run of the *20th Century Limited* glides along the Hudson River at Cold Spring, N.Y., behind J-3a No. 5453 in June 1938. NYC PHOTO; NYCSHS COLLECTION

Long-distance "PT" tenders were mated to the streamlined Hudsons beginning in 1943. These could scoop water "on the fly" like the original tenders, but their size meant that coaling stops between Buffalo and Harmon were no longer required. Grimy No. 5445 was at Elkhart, Indiana, in March 1945. JOE SCHMITZ COLLECTION

FACING PAGE, TOP: Most closely associated with the *Century* and other NYC fleet leaders, the streamlined Hudsons also locked couplers with more varied consists. No. 5449 led a head-end-heavy westbound near Sandusky, Ohio, in 1939. ANDREW HRITZ; JAY WILLIAMS COLLECTION

ABOVE: No. 5448 led an eastbound mixture of lightweight and heavyweight cars—probably the *Commodore Vanderbilt*—at Englewood, Illinois, in 1944. JAY WILLIAMS COLLECTION

The *20th Century Limited*, behind J-3a No. 5453, was westbound at Peekskill, N.Y., in 1938. NYC PHOTO; NYCSHS COLLECTION

The Evolving Hiawathas

So resounding was the public's embrace of the *Hiawathas* (see Chapter 2) that the Milwaukee Road was obliged to completely re-equip the expanding fleet, for the third time, in late 1938.

"Newest and greatest of a distinguished series of super-speed streamliners," is how the road billed the 1939 edition of its *Hiawatha*.

The brochure announcing the new equipment continued, "The original *Hiawatha* in 1935, the *Hiawatha* of 1937, and now this brand new Speedliner represent three distinct steps in the evolution of railroad trains. ... Every detail of the 1939 *Hiawatha*, from the illuminated station announcer in the Tip Top Tap to the rearward facing sofa in the observation lounge of the finned beaver-tail parlor car,

is carefully planned to make this train fit *your* needs and ideals in rail travel."

The 35 cars delivered by the company's hometown shops through that summer permitted all-new nine-car *Hiawatha* consists to enter Chicago–Twin Cities service on September 19, 1938. All together, two mail cars, four express-tap room cars, 15 coaches, four diners, six parlors (with drawing room), and four beaver-tail par-

lor-observation cars were built, along with 26 assorted lightweight cars intended to modernize service on other Milwaukee Road routes.

The new, third-generation *Hiawatha* cars were styled by Otto Kuhler in conjunction with the railroad's design staff. The cars were identifiable at a glance from their predecessors by their seven horizontal side ribs and revised paint scheme. The ribs were a styling device, but also gave the thin Cor-Ten steel side panels some added stiffness.

The *Hiawatha's* colors were rearranged to have a dark maroon window band hide the individual "dots" of the windows when the consist was viewed as a whole, thereby adding to the train's streamlined look. The sides were entirely yellow below the windows. A narrower maroon band ran along the letterboard, separated from the window band by more yellow.

Kuhler's touch was evident in the porthole windows of the tap room—unusual window shapes would become something of a Milwaukee Road passenger car hallmark over the next decade. He also "speedlined" the rear of the new beaver-tail observation cars by appending intersecting horizontal and vertical fins to shield—but not obstruct— the large, low-slung rear windows.

The new nine-car *Hiawatha* consists actually weighed slightly less than the 1937 edition, but offered an increase in revenue seats from 291 to 300. The increase in *total* seating was even larger, from 464 to 499—both a far cry from the original seven-car 1935 *Hiawatha's* 238 revenue and 376 total seats.

Trucks on the 1938 cars, designed once again by Karl Nystrom, were greatly improved over those applied to the earlier consists, primarily through the elimination of leaf springs and the introduction of hydraulic damping struts. The distinctive underbody equipment shrouds of the 1937 cars were reprised, but in an extended form that left no visual gaps between a car's trucks. Retractable steps and full-width diaphragms furthered the cars' col-

AUTHOR'S COLLECTION

The 1939 *Hiawatha* was all new, from the Kuhler-styled F-7 Hudson up front to the consist of nine rib-sided cars. MILWAUKEE ROAD PHOTO; TLC PUBLISHING COLLECTION

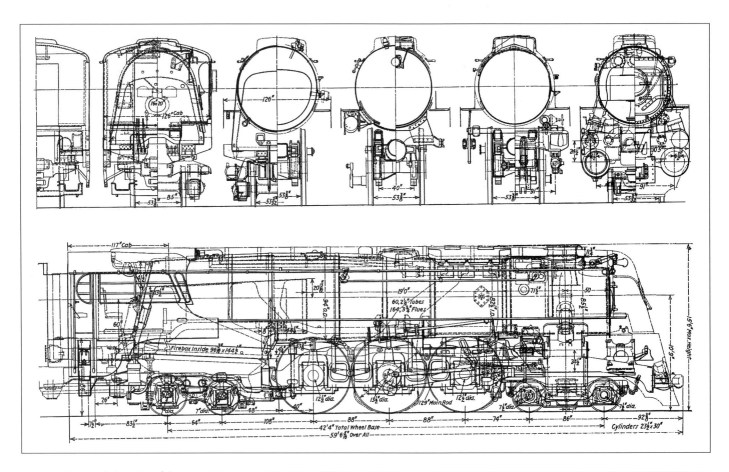

Cross sections and elevation of the Milwaukee Road F-7 Hudson.
RAILWAY AGE

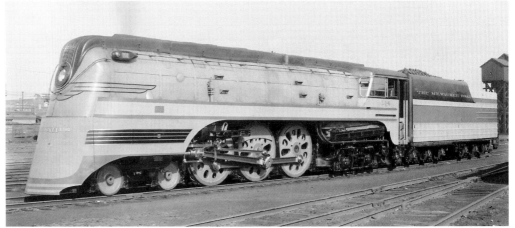

The F-7s were built by Alco and styled by Otto Kuhler—a worthy pedigree. Brand-new No. 104 was photographed at Chicago in September 1938. DANIEL PETERSON; TLC PUBLISHING COLLECTION

The engineer's side of No. 104, at Milwaukee on September 22, 1940. As planning got underway for the *Hiawatha's* 1939 re-equipping, consideration was given to employing diesels instead of steam. The railroad opted to wait until 1941 before purchasing diesels for passenger service: a pair of Electro-Motive E6A's and a pair of Alco DL-109s. The latter model was styled by none other than Otto Kuhler.
JAY WILLIAMS COLLECTION

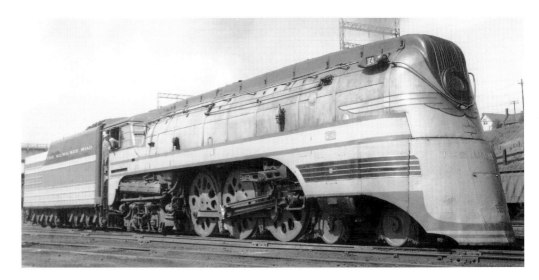

As far removed from *Hiawatha* duty as it could get, F-7 No. 101 breaks in on a freight on August 28, 1938. Elements within the Milwaukee Road tried to peg these 4-6-4s as the "Baltic" type, but most referred to them as Hudsons.
JAY WILLIAMS COLLECTION

Kuhler dropped the skyline casing on these engines down over the nose to a termination at the headlight. It was a treatment he had used before—on the GM&N *Rebel* power car—and would use again on the Alco DL-109.
MILWAUKEE ROAD PHOTO;
TLC PUBLISHING COLLECTION

lective aerodynamics. The new cars' roof cross-section was simplified with a more circular edge radius to reduce construction cost and complexity.

Metal interior trim was dispensed with in the new cars in favor of extensive use of native woods like walnut and maple for wall panels, interior window frames, and other trim. Sound attenuation was improved, and the railroad boasted that the 1939 *Hiawatha* was "quiet as a broadcasting studio … smooth as a gull on the wing."

Delivered at the same time, but not intended solely for the Chicago–Twin Cities *Hiawathas*, were six coal-fired Class

The original four Class A Atlantics also pulled the 1939 *Hiawatha* equipment—witness No. 4 at Chicago. JAY WILLIAMS COLLECTION

More typical of Class A assignments after the F-7 Hudsons arrived was No. 1's employment on the *North Woods Hiawatha*. The train is leaving the outskirts of Wauwatosa, Wis., in this postwar view. RICHARD J. COOK, JAY WILLIAMS COLLECTION

F-7 streamlined Hudsons (Nos. 100-105). Built by Alco, they were "Speedlined by Otto Kuhler"—and sported plaques on their cylinder skirts that said so. The locomotives' initial assignments included Chicago–Twin Cities service on the *Olympian* and the *Pioneer Limited* (as well as on the *Hiawatha* when traffic warranted), and beyond Minneapolis to Harlowton, Montana, on the *Olympian*.

The veteran Atlantics could still cope with the latest *Hiawatha* consists, and had their tender livery modified to blend with the 1939 cars' revised paint arrangement.

Elements of the new Hudsons' shrouding design—particularly the way in which the skyline casing flowed down over the top of the nose and into the headlight bezel—were straight out of conceptual sketches prepared by Kuhler earlier in the decade and published in *Portraits of the Iron Horse* (Rand McNally, 1937). Kuhler had already applied this particular styling trait to the power car of the 1935 GM&N *Rebel*, and would adapt it again for Alco's DL-109 of 1940.

Although Kuhler was on record as preferring streamlining that maintained a steam locomotive's "basic form," the general lines of the Class A shrouds were retained, with less-comprehensive running gear skirts and the aforementioned skyline casing the major physical differences on the F-7s. Kuhler accentuated the Hudsons' greater length by applying bold striping to the cylinder skirts and running boards, stretching the stainless steel nose wings, and painting the skyline casing black. The vertical, chromed grill above the recessed headlight admitted air for smoke-lifting, while the stack was subtly accented by a low-profile cap, barely visible above the skyline. The lower portion of the pilot shroud was painted maroon in a manner that reduced its apparent bulk. The vestibule-type cab looked more like a greenhouse, with its expanse of wraparound glazing. The sides of the tenders were partially ribbed and painted to match the newly delivered *Hiawatha* equipment.

The Hudsons' Boxpok drivers were the same considerable diameter—84 inches—as the Atlantics'. Working on 300 PSI boiler pressure, the F-7s exerted 50,300 pounds of tractive effort. All engine axles were equipped with roller bearings. The F-7s' tenders rode on six-wheel trucks, carrying 25 tons of coal and 20,000 gallons of water.

Hiawatha motive power garnered a great deal of attention, but the trains' rear end was just as interesting. Kuhler added an assembly of fins to the observation car of the 1939 *Hiawatha*, but the "beaver tail" profile was largely unchanged from its 1935 introduction. JAY WILLIAMS COLLECTION

The collection of Pacifics streamlined by Otto Kuhler for the Lehigh Valley railroad in 1939 were an amalgam from the designer's "bag of tricks"—a bit of B&O *Royal Blue* here, a little Milwaukee Road beaver-tail there. They were, arguably, his best work. LV PHOTO; AUTHOR'S COLLECTION

KUHLER'S GEMS

The Lehigh Valley was one of the Northeast's perennial second-stringers, laboring for freight and passenger traffic alike in the shadow of larger and usually wealthier neighbors like the Pennsy and New York Central, the Lackawanna, and the Erie. The Lehigh Valley pinned its existence on the hard, clean-burning coal extracted from the hills of eastern Pennsylvania, and for that reason was known as "The Route of the Black Diamond."

Lehigh Valley's long-distance passenger operations connected Newark, N.J., and Buffalo via Wilkes-Barre (Pa.). The Pennsy forwarded LV passengers between Newark and Manhattan's Pennsylvania Station. Cornell University at Ithaca, N.Y., and other on-line colleges provided a welcome source of traffic, but not enough to forestall a precipitous overall decline during the depression.

Otto Kuhler was an acquaintance of LV President Duncan Kerr, and in 1938 the designer was commissioned to revamp a gas-electric car in the hope of building traffic between Newark and Mauch Chunk, Pennsylvania. The gas-electric was a prelude to the *Asa Packer*, a four-car day train of modernized heavyweights led by a "cleanlined"—but not streamlined—Pacific. Named to honor the road's first

president, the *Asa Packer* was christened at Bethlehem, Pa., on January 31, 1939, and entered revenue service the following day. A striking yellow-and-black livery did much to update the appearance of the essentially unmodernized cars and locomotive. Pacific No. 2023 was given only modest running board skirts and a sheet-metal "chin" between pilot and smokebox. A matching Pacific, No. 2022, was outshopped in April 1939 to permit double-daily service aimed at New York World's Fair visitors.

Having boosted the public profile of LV's passenger trains, the *Asa Packer* was merely a taste of things to come. Kerr and Kuhler had turned their attention to a more extensive streamlining of the LV's steam-powered passenger trains.

The *John Wilkes* was christened on June 2, 1939, at a ceremony in Wilkes-Barre. The name, selected by Kerr, honored an 18th century British parliamentarian, author, and champion of Colonial American rights. The train's streamlined Pacific and all but one of its nine modernized—but unstreamlined—heavyweight cars were the product of LV's Sayre (Pa.) shops, and workers there had been invited to enjoy the fruits of their craftsmanship on a pre-inaugural run through New York's Finger Lakes region. Over 8,000 potential passengers also visited the train at Hazleton (Pa.), Wilkes-Barre, and Jersey City prior to its official inauguration. Duncan Kerr, responsible for bringing Otto Kuhler into the Lehigh Valley fold, was stricken during one of the preview runs and died before his brainchild had turned a revenue wheel.

The *John Wilkes'* June 4, 1939, entry into revenue service between Newark and Wilkes-Barre was well-timed for World's Fair traffic. The original consist included a baggage-express car, four coaches, a buffet-lounge "club" car, a diner, and a Pullman-operated parlor. The parlor—the former *Emerald*, renamed *John Wilkes* for its new assignment—was the only car not refurbished at Sayre, the work being performed instead by Pullman-Standard in Worcester, Massachusetts.

President Kerr had selected black and red as the new train's signature, honoring on-line Cornell's school colors. A broad black band extended from the locomotive back through the cars' window area. Sides above and below the windows were Cornell red, accented by white pinstriping. Roofs were black.

While the train's heavyweight cars harked to the *Asa Packer*, the *John Wilkes'* locomotives were classic Kuhler. K-5 Pacifics Nos. 2101 and 2102 were Baldwin products dating back to 1916, but Kuhler

drew from his growing repertoire to make them the equal of any streamlined locomotives in service then or after. A bullet nose, with centered headlight, brought to mind his work on B&O 5304 for the *Royal Blue*. The assembly of horizontal and vertical "speedline" fins between the the LV engines' pilot and smokebox were pure 1939 *Hiawatha* beaver-tail. A low skyline casing and abundant stainless steel pinstriping gave the Pacifics a windswept look. The headlight bezel was in the form of a stainless steel diamond, evoking the railroad's herald and hinting at a decor element repeated in the car interiors. The cab windows, curved at their forward end and divided into three horizontal panels,

BELOW: Red-and-black K-6-S Pacific No. 2093 bore the *Black Diamond's* name on its tender.
TLC PUBLISHING COLLECTION

BOTTOM: K-5 No. 2102 was streamlined for the *John Wilkes*, and its tender lettered accordingly. The horizontal fins at the front of the *John Wilkes* engines were not truncated as they were on the later *Black Diamond* Pacifics.
TLC PUBLISHING COLLECTION

TOP: K-6-S No. 2097 has an eight-car *Black Diamond* in tow, including two of the "American Flyer"-style lightweight coaches. TLC PUBLISHING COLLECTION

ABOVE: Lehigh Valley's third streamlined K-6-S was No. 2089. TLC PUBLISHING COLLECTION

A group of five 92-seat lightweight coaches was obtained from Pullman-Standard in the fall of 1939, along with a similar number of 82-seaters incorporating a large women's lounge. Resembling the "American Flyer" cars pioneered by the New Haven Railroad, LV Nos. 1510-1519 differed most obviously in having squared-off roof ends. The exterior paint on these cars and the heavyweights modernized for *Black Diamond* service mirrored the *John Wilkes'* colors and layout.

Launched with typical fanfare in April 1940, each of the two re-equipped *Black Diamond* consists included a heavyweight baggage-RPO and three of the P-S lightweight coaches along with a modernized diner, parlor, lounge, and parlor-observation for the daylight trip across the main line. The spare P-S coaches were employed on the *John Wilkes*, with its modernized cars reassigned to the *Asa Packer* (marking the demise of Kuhler's yellow-and-black livery on that train).

Class K-6-S Pacifics Nos. 2089, 2093, and 2097 were selected for streamlining and assignment to the *Black Diamond*. The first had been homebuilt at Sayre in 1925, while the other two had been delivered by Alco in 1924. The trio emerged as near-copies of the Pacifics styled for the *John Wilkes*, but with slight refinements in the shrouding around the stack and between the pilot and smokebox. Also absent was the sweeping front-end handrail treatment, replaced by abbreviated vertical holds above the pilot beam. The train name, though, did appear on the tender.

Wartime austerity saw the group of five streamlined LV Pacifics lose their stainless trim and intricate paint schemes. Solid black with a single wide red stripe became the new norm.

Diesels came to the Lehigh Valley's passenger operation in the form of 14 Alco PA-1s (Nos. 601-614) in early 1948. By June 20 of that year, the Alcos had unceremoniously bumped steam from LV's intercity schedules.

The displaced Pacifics were sent back to Sayre to have Kuhler's marvelous streamlining removed, after which they were assigned to menial duties across the railroad. By December 1951 the LV had completely dieselized and the last of the once-streamlined speedsters had been scrapped.

became an integral part of the striping that extended across the upper tender and onto the consist. The railroad's name was rendered in three-dimensional chrome lettering on the narrow running board skirts and on the sides of the tender's coal bunker. The train name, in bold script, appeared on the tender.

Mechanically, the two Pacifics had been rebuilt at Sayre with Boxpok drivers, new valve gear, and alloy-steel drive rods.

As the *John Wilkes* was taking shape, plans were underway to effect a similar streamlining of Lehigh Valley's Newark–Buffalo flagship, the *Black Diamond*. Going one better than a mere heavyweight facelift, the re-equipped *Black Diamond* would incorporate both modernized and new rolling stock.

TOWARD A STREAMLINED STANDARD

When the time came to inaugurate its re-equipped *Broadway Limited* on June 15, 1938, the Pennsylvania Railroad had but one streamlined steam locomotive on the property, compared to rival New York Central's eleven.

Pennsy's sleek GG-1 electrics filled the press photographers' viewfinders as the "Fleet of Modernism" was launched under wire in New York and Philadelphia. In Chicago, Raymond Loewy's voluptuously shrouded Pacific No. 3768 (see Chapter 2) was front and center as the first streamlined *Broadway Limited* departed for New York. The streamlined K-4s became a regular on the west end of the *Broadway's* New York–Chicago run. The Pacific's unshrouded rostermates handled the "Fleet of Modernism" and "Blue Ribbon Fleet"—the latter were Pennsy's lesser-light intercity passenger trains—west of Harrisburg (Pa.), beyond the limits of the road's recently extended electrified zone.

Unlike NYC's *20th Century Limited*, the streamlined *Broadway* was not a completely lightweight train. Pennsy opted to modernize two heavyweight dining cars, and these blended with the new P-S cars as best they could by virtue of Loewy's paint scheme and some judicious cosmetic sheet metal. The rest of the re-equipped train had *Cascade*, *Imperial*, *County*, and *City*-series cars in common with the *Century*. *Harbor Springs* and *Harbor Point* were the 1938 *Broadway's* mid-train sleeper-lounge cars, with keystone-shaped tail signs gracing round-ended, 2-drawing room, 1-bedroom, buffet-lounge-observations *Skyline View* and *Metropolitan View*.

An additional 82 lightweight cars—mostly sleepers and mostly from Pullman-Standard—were delivered to the Pennsy between 1937 and 1939 in order to fully or partially re-equip other members of the "Fleet of Modernism." These included the *Spirit of St. Louis* (New York–Washington, DC–St. Louis), the *General* (New York–Chicago), the *Liberty Limited* (Washington, DC–Chicago), the *Pittsburgher* (New York–Pittsburgh), and the *Golden Triangle* (Chicago–Pittsburgh). An all-coach, eight-car train of modernized heavyweights joined the fleet as the New York–Chicago *Trail Blazer* on July 28, 1939. It was launched on the same day as, and in competition with, NYC's similarly equipped *Pacemaker*.

Deciding, for the moment, not to create additional shrouded K-4s Pacifics to lead his "Fleet of Modernism" streamliners, Pennsy President Martin W. Clement announced within days of the streamlined *Broadway's* debut that his railroad,

Pennsylvania Railroad S-1 No. 6100 was initially lettered AMERICAN RAILROADS for its display at the New York World's Fair. PRR PHOTO; TLC PUBLISHING COLLECTION

in conjunction with the engineering staffs of builders Alco, Lima, and Baldwin, was working to develop an entirely new class of streamlined steam locomotive for heavy passenger service. Chief among their goals was a locomotive capable of moving a 14-car train at a sustained 100 MPH. A 4-4-4-4 duplex-drive wheel arrangement was proposed, with a 12-wheeled tender carrying 26 tons of coal and 25,000 gallons of water.

Dubbed the "Pennsylvania Type" in contemporary press releases, the proposed design would become the shark-nosed T-1 of 1942 (see Chapter 4).

Pennsy, the trio of commercial builders, and Loewy made headlines in the interim with what proved to be an evolutionary step toward the T-1—streamlined Class S-1 duplex-drive 6-4-4-6 No. 6100, built by the PRR and unveiled in the spring of 1939.

Each of the two sets of four-coupled, 84-inch Baldwin disc drivers was powered by its own set of 22x26-inch cylinders. Each set of cylinders, in turn, had their own exhaust piping and stack. Weight on drivers was 281,440 pounds, with a total engine weight of 608,170 pounds. Steam pressure was 300 PSI. The engine's rated

tractive force was 76,400 pounds. The fully loaded tender, with its two eight-wheel Buckeye trucks, weighed in at 451,840 pounds. The welded tender could hold 26.5 tons of coal and 24,230 gallons of water. All axles were equipped with roller bearings.

The centerpiece of the railroad exhibit at the 1939 New York World's Fair, PRR No. 6100 was a sleek monster, over 140 feet long—eight feet longer than a Union Pacific "Big Boy"—that exuded speed even when standing still. Loewy was at the top of his form with this one-of-a-kind giant.

Similar in basic form to K-4s No. 3768, the streamlined shroud designed by Loewy for No. 6100 had an elongated and "windswept" front-end treatment that complemented, and even accentuated, the S-1's much greater length. Loewy returned to NYU's wind tunnel to perfect the design. The aluminum smokebox cover fitted to No. 6100 was bullet-shaped in contrast to the Pacific's hemisphere. A horizontal wedge curved back from either side of the protruding headlight case and trailed into a trim molding running the length of engine and tender. No. 6100's pilot shrouding was more pronounced than its predecessor's, giving the look of a jutting, squared chin. An angled prow bridged the deep notch between the top of the pilot and the underside of the bullet nose. Smoke lifting was accomplished in the same manner as with No. 3768, wherein an airflow was directed over the top of the boiler and around the stack (without the use of a grilled intake as had become the standard on other roads). Deep, flat skirts—removed in later years—managed to keep most of the 6-4-4-6's running gear visible.

Treatment of the vestibule-type aluminum cab exterior was strongly reminiscent of the PRR's GG-1 electric—or, rather, half of one. On the S-1, a taut diaphragm concealed what little gap remained between engine and tender. The tender itself was deeply skirted, with a roofline that was faired very smoothly from the engine's cab height down to the typical car's roof level. Metal trim striping ran from the pilot to the rear of the tender just above the running gear.

Given its World's Fair status as an ambassador for the industry, the S-1 was lettered AMERICAN RAILROADS while on display. And what a display it was—No. 6100, weighing almost 500 tons, was mounted atop a custom-built, sunken treadmill. Under its own steam, the S-1's drivers rotated to turn a roller assembly. This was connected by V-belts to other rollers, fore and aft, that turned the pilot truck and trailing truck wheels at the same velocity. The driving axles' rollers were linked by another V-belt to traction motors which, used as generators, energized motors rotating the tender wheels and provided a mechanical load to the engine. The remarkable display was an immediate hit with Fairgoers.

Following its time in the national spotlight, Pennsy's solitary S-1 was evaluated at the Altoona Test Plant and in service on the "Fleet of Modernism." With a rigid wheelbase too long to negotiate tight curves in Pittsburgh, No. 6100 spent most of its career between the division point of Crestline, Ohio, and Chicago.

Loewy made a point of seeing his creation in action, and described an encounter at Fort Wayne, Indiana, in his 1979 book, *Industrial Design*: "It flashed by like a steel thunderbolt, the ground shaking under me, a blast of air that almost sucked me into its whirlwind. Approximately a million pounds of locomotive were crashing through near me. I felt shaken and overwhelmed by an unforgettable feeling of power, by a sense of pride at the sight of what I had helped create in a quick sketch six inches wide on a scrap of paper. For the first time, perhaps, I realized that I had contributed something to a great nation that had taken me in ... ."

No. 6100 paved the way for what would become the largest class of streamlined steam locomotives in America, the Pennsy T-1.

The orphaned S-1, alas, went to the scrapper in 1949.

During the war, the entire area of skirting below No. 6100's running boards was removed. The S-1 has a heavyweight consist in tow at Englewood in this winter view.
AUTHOR'S COLLECTION

Baltimore & Ohio's *Cincinnatian*—shown on October 12, 1949, at Bond, Md.—was a notable exception to the postwar trend of diesel-powered streamliners. The rebuilt heavyweight cars and streamlined Pacifics were products of the B&O's Mount Clare shops. WILLIAM P. PRICE

War erupted in Europe in September 1939, but it would be another 15 months before the United States was drawn into the conflict. Just as the financial turmoil of the 1930s was receding, more shifts in the political and cultural landscape were emerging. The 1940s, clearly, would be a tumultuous decade. For their part, America's railroads would undergo a seismic upheaval.

By the time the New York World's Fair opened for its second season at Flushing Meadows in the spring of 1940, the American public had embraced—and had come to expect—streamlined forms as an integral part of their everyday lives.

Examples of the industrial designers' efforts were visible at every turn—in the home, at the workplace, in retail and leisure establishments. More and more Americans were able to afford personal automobiles, and those vehicles invariably were the visual offspring of Walter Chrysler's 1934 "Airflow."

The impact of the public's newfound mobility was a festering sore for the railroads—the momentum had been gathering since 1929, and the parade of re-equipped trains of the mid- and late 1930s appeared, at best, to check the infection. Lessons had been learned, some painfully. The inflexibility of the early articulated trainsets to meet traffic fluctuations or to permit efficient shop work made them pioneering orphans. Streamliners made up of individual cars, just as Bel Geddes had proposed in 1931, had become the new standard. Cars could be added, or removed, virtually anywhere, at anytime, for any reason, just as they had been in the "old days" of the heavyweight era.

The railroads, obviously, wanted the public to fill their trains, and the public wanted—expected—streamliners. Perish the railroad passenger department that balked at giving its customers what they deserved. Passengers would take their business elsewhere, and competing railroads could, and frequently did, move in for the kill by soliciting their rivals' "deprived" passengers.

Buses, automobiles, and the emerging airlines were the common foe, but affected individual railroads in different ways. Operators of trains serving Florida from the Northeast and Midwest, for example, launched a number of all-coach streamliners in 1939 and 1940—some steam-powered—intended not so much to appeal to air travelers as to win back budget traffic lost to the highways. A colorful decade lay ahead.

A New Angle

When the 1940s dawned, the Frisco's Kansas City–Tulsa–Oklahoma City (Okla.) *Firefly* was just three weeks old, having been inaugurated on December 10, 1939. The pair of four-car trains each included a baggage-mail car, a baggage-mail-coach, a deluxe coach, and a diner-lounge—all

Frisco's eastbound *Firefly* pauses at Sapulpa, Oklahoma, on its Kansas City–Oklahoma City journey behind one of three Pacifics given this distinctive streamlined shroud. FRISCO PHOTO, AUTHOR'S COLLECTION

heavyweights refurbished and modernized to varying degrees at the road's Springfield (Mo.) shops. They emerged in a blue-and-silver paint scheme, with black roofs.

The *Firefly's* schedule demanded an average speed of 52 MPH over the 379-mile route. To power the high-speed *Firefly*, a trio of 29-year-old Pacifics was sent to Springfield shops to be upgraded and streamlined. Nos. 1018, 1026, and 1031 had been built by Baldwin in 1910.

The shroud design chosen went sufficiently beyond "bullet-nosed" that it is invariably described as "sinister-looking." A jacket enveloped the boiler and its upper protrusions and tapered into a pointed snout. Smooth pilot sheathing extended up to the underside of the nose cone, and the ends of the pilot beam were wrapped by skirts that flowed up and into the edge of the running board without obscuring the running gear. The front of the cab was faired into the boiler jacket at a shallow angle, and underbody skirting was added to the tender. Above the smokebox, where the boiler jacket curved down to form the top of the nose cone, a wind-splitting, flat-topped prow jutted out ahead of the stack. Recessed into this prow's knife-edge was the locomotive's steam whistle; jauntily mounted just ahead of that was the brass bell. Boiler jacket, nose, pilot shroud, cab, and tender were painted dark blue. The running board skirts were aluminum, edged in red, and led into a stripe across the tender sides. The engines' number and road name were lettered within the aluminum stripe. Sinister, perhaps, but looking rather more like a big, blue armadillo from certain angles, the streamlining on these three locomotives was unique.

Similar striping, minus the shroud, was also applied to some Frisco 4-8-2s used in Ozark Mountain passenger service.

SPECIAL DUTY

During the late 1930s, before improved roads and widespread automobile ownership expanded their travel options, vacationers often relied on special trains to reach their holiday destinations. Seasonal trains like the *East Wind*, the *Mountaineer*, and the *Valley Flyer* were among the last of a breed soon rendered extinct by postwar personal mobility. The latter two were collections of brightly painted, but unstreamlined, equipment and are discussed on page 130. The *East Wind*, though, was very much a streamliner.

The *East Wind* debuted in June 1940 as a first-class coach train conveying vacationers from Washington, DC, and New York City to Bangor, Maine. Billed as "The first deluxe all-coach train to Maine and New Hampshire," its 705-mile journey traversed the rails of the PRR, New Haven, Boston & Maine,

This leaflet was issued in 1940 to promote the first season of the *East Wind*. AUTHOR'S COLLECTION

The *East Wind* was on Boston & Maine rails, behind B&M Pacific No. 3712, on July 13, 1940, less than a month into the train's first season of operation between Washington, DC, New York City, and points in New Hampshire and Maine. The specially painted consist included a New Haven baggage car, PRR coaches, a New Haven grill car, and a leased ACL diner. BOB'S PHOTOS

Streamstyled Louisville & Nashville Pacific No. 295 leads the *South Wind* near Lebanon Junction, Kentucky, in 1941. The seven-car Budd coach train ran between Chicago and Miami on a PRR-L&N-ACL-FEC route. Pennsy and L&N both operated streamlined steam locomotives on this train. L&N PHOTO; JAY WILLIAMS COLLECTION

and Maine Central. Northbound trips ran every day from June 21, 1940, through September 13, with southbound dates of operation in the first season were June 22 through September 14. The 7:00 am departure from Washington Union Station got passengers to Rockland (Me.) at 8:40 pm and Bangor at 9:30 pm—on weekends, the train ran only as far as Portland (Me.), with a 6:10 pm arrival. The homeward trek offered a 6:45 am daily departure from Bangor and a 10:05 pm arrival in Washington, with 18 intermediate stops.

Equipment for the seasonal consist— sourced from the New Haven, B&M, and Pennsy, along with a leased Atlantic Coast Line diner—was painted in a special canary-yellow, silver, and blue color scheme in the train's first two seasons. So strong was the demand for space on the daylight train that additional cars were added after only a few trips had been made. The *East Wind's* semi-streamlined, reclining-seat coaches were supplemented by a grill car and a tavern-lounge.

The *East Wind* traveled under Pennsy and New Haven catenary between the nation's capital and New Haven (Conn.). From that point northward, the train was pulled by steam power from the respective railroads' general passenger pools.

The *East Wind* was reprised for the 1941 and 1942 summer seasons—the latter without special paint—and returned after a wartime hiatus.

GROUP EFFORTS

Not until 1940 did a streamlined steam locomotive call the South "home." The multiple-operator streamlined trains that had been plying the rails between Washington, DC, and Florida since 1939 had done so behind either diesels or unstreamlined steam.

It was to connect with the main section of one of these, the dieselized New York–Miami *Silver Meteor*, that the Seaboard Air Line (SAL) shrouded three 1913-vintage Class P Pacifics in early 1940. SAL Nos. 865, 867, and 868 were clad in shovel-nosed shrouds decorated with the bright "citrus" colors worn by the road's Electro-Motive E4 diesels. The nose treatment of the Pacifics' shrouds bore more than a passing resemblance to the diesels' slanted profile, although the green, orange, yellow, and red stripes were arranged differently. The trio of Pacifics protected the St. Petersburg–Wildwood (Fla.) section of the *Silver Meteor*.

Also important to the Florida trade were the multiple-operator trains that connected Chicago and the Midwest with the Sunshine State.

At the end of 1940, nine railroads operating three Chicago–Florida passenger routes coordinated the introduction of three new streamlined all-coach trains. Each of the three reserved-seat trains traveled over its own distinct route, and by arranging every-third-day departures, an overall daily service was provided. Passengers were given the flexibility of leaving on one of the three routes and returning via another, if they desired. Outwardly individualistic, the trio of streamliners offered similar amenities and interior layouts. The *Dixie Flagler*, the *City of Miami*, and the *South Wind* were inaugurated over a three-day period beginning on December 17, 1940.

Of the 1.5 million visitors traveling between Chicago and Florida in 1939, surveys indicated that almost three-quarters went by bus or automobile. The nine partnering railroads were determined to increase their share of the market, and staged lavish pre-inaugural festivities and beauty-queen laden sendoffs for the three new trains. Just as the three sets of equipment were similar but not identical, so were the trains' christenings. The *Dixie Flagler's* observation car was drenched with a bottle of Florida orange juice; the *City of Miami* ceremony employed bottled water from Biscayne Bay; and "Miss South Wind" dispatched her namesake with a bottle of traditional champagne.

Despite having routes of differing mileage, all three trains maintained the same 29.5-hour end-to-end schedule—more than a two-hour improvement over the previous best—with a 9:40 am Chicago departure getting passengers to Miami at 4:10 pm the next day. Northbound trains departed Miami at 6:25 pm—after only a two-and-a-quarter-hour layover—and arrived in Chicago at 10:25 pm the following evening. End-to-end mileages

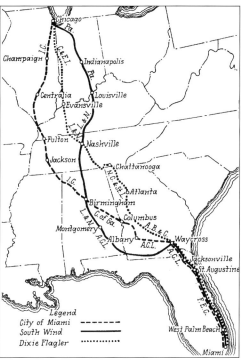

Seaboard Air Line streamlined three Class P Pacifics in 1940 to handle connections for diesel-powered mainline streamliners. No. 868 was at St. Petersburg, Fla., on November 4, 1940. TLC PUBLISHING COLLECTION

Chicago to Florida in 1940. RAILWAY AGE

Louisville & Nashville Pacific No. 277 was streamlined in 1940 for service on the *Dixie Flagler*. By the time of this September 1946 view at East St. Louis, Ill., it was being used on the *Georgian*. HAROLD K. VOLLRATH COLLECTION

for the three routes were: *Dixie Flagler*, 1,434; *City of Miami*, 1,493; and *South Wind*, 1,559. Accordingly, the *South Wind* had to maintain the highest average speed, 52.8 MPH. Only one consist of each train was needed to protect the coordinated schedule.

Illinois Central assigned an Electro-Motive E-unit to its *City of Miami*, but the other two trains were powered, for the most part, by an exotic collection of streamlined steam locomotives.

The *Dixie Flagler* was a seven-car Budd stainless steel train owned by the Florida East Coast (FEC). It departed from Chicago's Dearborn Station and operated over six different partner railroads on its way south: the Chicago & Eastern Illinois (C&EI) to Evansville (Ind.); Louisville & Nashville (L&N) to Nashville; Nashville, Chattanooga & St. Louis (NC&StL) to Atlanta; Atlanta, Birmingham & Coast (AB&C) to Waycross (Ga.); Atlantic Coast Line (ACL) to Jacksonville (Fla.); and finally over FEC's home rails to Miami. The AB&C was merged into the ACL in 1945, reducing the partner roster by one.

The original *Dixie Flagler* consist had been built in 1939 for operation between Jacksonville and Miami as the *Henry M. Flagler*, its name honoring the father of Florida development. As delivered, it comprised baggage-dormitory-coach *Stuart*; hostess room-coach *Delray Beach*; diner *Fort Lauderdale*; coaches *Hobe Sound*, *Hollywood*, and *Melbourne*; and round-ended tavern-observation *Lake Worth*.

While FEC employed the *Henry M. Flagler's* Electro-Motive E6 to lead the *Dixie Flagler* and ACL typically used an unstreamlined Pacific, partners C&EI, L&N, and AB&C opted to shroud existing steam engines for the new high-profile train. As initially outshopped, the skyline casings and bullet nose variations applied to the collection of streamlined Pacifics gave them an extended-family appearance.

North-end anchor C&EI contributed black-and-silver K-2 Pacific No. 1008 to the cause, but the engine lost its original *Daylight*-like front-end styling after a collision. The locomotive entered *Dixie Flagler* service following repairs, but with its conical smokebox front replaced by a V-striped shovel nose. Broad running board skirts were retained, but their striping arrangement was altered to conform to the new nose treatment.

For its part, L&N's South Louisville shops applied a skyline casing, deep running board skirts, a conical headlight housing, and the same red-and-yellow-trimmed, black-and-silver colors to Class K-5 Pacific No. 277, a product of Alco originally delivered in 1924.

NC&StL's Nashville shop forces produced the least-streamlined of the Pacifics refitted for *Dixie Flagler* service. Class K-2d No. 536 was given just running board skirts, pilot sheeting, and a skyline casing. Even the special paint—matching the L&N and C&EI engines—couldn't compensate for a cluttered smokebox front and the decidedly unstreamlined Vanderbilt tender.

The most obscure of the steam locomotives streamlined for *Dixie Flagler* service was Pacific No. 79 of the Atlanta, Birmingham & Coast. Built by Alco in 1913, the Class J-1 engine rode on 69-inch drivers and exerted 32,500 pounds of tractive force. Preparation for its *Dixie Flagler* assignment included an enlarged tender. Skirting, headlight housing, and skyline casing generally resembled those adopted by L&N, but the AB&C engine was painted in a bright yellow-and-red scheme

BELOW: Originally streamlined with a conical nose resembling its L&N *Dixie Flagler* routemates, Chicago & Eastern Illinois K-2 No. 1008 was rebuilt with this flat nose following a collision. The engine was photographed at Chicago in April 1942. All work was done at the C&EI's Oaklawn shops in Danville, Illinois. By mid-1946, No. 1008—displaced by new EMD E7s—had lost its streamlining altogether and was reassigned. The Baldwin dated to 1911.

BOTTOM: Atlanta, Birmingham & Coast No. 79 was streamlined for its part of the *Dixie Flagler* route, and modified in 1941 with this hemispherical nose and smooth boiler jacket. It was painted in FEC-inspired yellow and red.
BOTH, HAROLD K. VOLLRATH COLLECTION

designed by draftsman Joseph Gentry and inspired by partner FEC's E-units. Against an overall red background, a broad yellow band swept up from the pilot and was carried back along the running board skirting and across the cab and tender.

AB&C No. 79's streamlining was enhanced in December 1941 with the addition of a hemispherical nose, additional sheet metal above the pilot, and a clean-up of the boiler jacket. In both iterations, the train name was lettered in black towards the front of the running board skirts. Other lettering, revised slightly with the cosmetic alterations, was rendered in aluminum paint. No. 79 weathered the war with its streamlining intact, only to be destroyed in a head-on collision while leading the *Dixie Flagler* near Talbotton, Georgia, on July 4, 1945.

The AB&C was merged into ACL at the end of 1945, and for a time thereafter the expanded ACL portion of the *Dixie Flagler's* run was still led by steam. ACL often assigned 4-8-2s to the train, which regularly included heavyweight and other "foreign" cars during and shortly after the war.

The third of the Chicago–Florida coach streamliners of December 1940 was the *South Wind*, its consist owned by the Pennsylvania Railroad. Despite being stainless steel products of the Budd Company, the seven fluted cars were painted in Pennsy's standard Tuscan red. In keeping with the *Dixie Flagler* and the P-S-built *City of Miami*, the original *South Wind* offered a baggage-dorm-coach, four full coaches, a diner, and a round-ended diner-lounge-observation car. The train left Chicago Union Station and traveled on Pennsy rails as far as Louisville. The L&N then forwarded the cars as far as Montgomery, Alabama. The *South Wind* ran over the ACL between Montgomery and Jacksonville, where FEC took over for the last leg into Miami.

As with the *Dixie Flagler*, FEC and ACL operated the *South Wind* with diesel and unstreamlined steam power, respectively. The L&N assigned streamlined Class K-7s Pacific No. 295 to the *South Wind*, wearing shrouding and paint similar to the *Dixie Flagler*-assigned No. 277. No. 295 had been built by Alco in 1925 to an experimental three-cylinder design, but was converted to two-cylinder configuration in the course of its 1940 overhaul for *South Wind* service. Another element

of the refit was the engine's mating with a tender carrying 20,000 gallons of water and 27 tons of coal, permitting non-stop running over the train's 205-mile Birmingham–Nashville segment. When No. 295 developed mechanical troubles in 1941, L&N streamlined a third Pacific, Class K-5 No. 275, as an interim black-and-silver replacement. Other unmodified L&N Pacifics substituted for their streamlined siblings on occasion.

After the war, L&N repainted No. 295 in two-tone Tuscan red, with gold striping and lettering, to blend with the Pennsy *South Wind* consist. Expanded consists soon eclipsed the Pacifics' power, however, and the arrival of General Motors E-units spelled their ultimate demise.

PROGRESSION ON THE PENNSY
For its share of *South Wind* mileage, as well as assignment to the *General*, the new, all-coach New York–Washington–St. Louis *Jeffersonian*, and other trains, the Pennsy tapped Raymond Loewy to streamline a quartet of K-4s Pacifics—Nos. 1120, 2665, 3678, and 5338. All were given smoothed pilots, hemispherical noses, low-profile skyline casings, and slab-like running board skirts that harked backed to elements of a 1935 proposal by New York-based industrial designer—and subsequent Loewy partner—C. Louis Otto.

Pronounced headlight bezels and PRR Keystone-shaped numberboards adorned the K-4s' rounded smokebox covers, with the overall effect being a

Streamlined K-4s No. 1120 was leading the *Chicago Arrow* into Englewood, Ill., in January 1944. Among this engine's original assignments after its 1940 restyling was the *South Wind*. JAY WILLIAMS COLLECTION

top: PRR K-4s No. 1120, on the
Broadway Limited in 1941.
HAROLD K. VOLLRATH COLLECTION

above: Wheel arrangement aside,
the similarity between C. Louis
Otto's 1935 conceptual rendering
and the 1940 PRR K-4s streamlining is remarkable. RAILWAY AGE

below: The *Trail Blazer*, behind
poppet-valve-equipped K-4s No.
3847 in June 1946. C. G. GIBB,
JAY WILLIAMS COLLECTION

somewhat disjointed assemblage of
streamlined substructures.

Loewy and Otto took locomotive
styling in a new direction with what they
termed the "prow-nose" Pennsy T-1 of
1942. The vertically pinched, tapered nose
and portholed skirt lost some of their cut-
ting edge when regarded against the back-
drop of Otto's portholed 1935 conceptual
rendering and his partner's contemporary
client base. Loewy's mid-1930s restyling of
the Virginia Ferry Corporation's Chesa-

peake Bay steamship *Princess Anne*
merged aerodynamics and marine architecture, and in 1939 Raymond Loewy
Associates was retained by the Panama
Line to design the interiors of new passenger liners *Ancon*, *Cristobal*, and *Panama*.
Elements of these marine commissions
could be seen in the styling for the duplex-
drive T-1 prototypes as Loewy's firm, and
Pennsy, sought to stay ahead of the pack.

Cosmetic styling of the T-1 design,
largely the work of Louis Otto, reverted to
Loewy's demonstrated preference for full
boiler shrouds in the place of narrow skyline casings. As Loewy saw them, full
shrouds were more effective in hiding "the
steel excrescences that formerly protruded
above the engine."

Intended to satisfy the same operational requirements as the S-1 of 1939—
that is, to emulate the performance
capabilities of the GG-1—prototype T-1s
Nos. 6110 and 6111 emerged from the
Baldwin plant in the spring of 1942. Their
long, shark-like prows jutted above a
bulky but similarly thrusting pilot shroud.
A closely spaced trio of portholes graced
each side of this pilot housing, which
flowed up into deep running board skirts.

More radical than the T-1s' styling,
though, was their 4-4-4-4 duplex-drive
configuration—designed to reduce the
weight of reciprocating parts associated

with a single set of cylinders. Vestibule type cabs and hulking, smoothsided tenders swept the locomotives' highly streamlined form into trailing consists as often as not comprising heavyweight cars.

Cosmetic changes altered the front-end styling of the 50 production T-1s of 1945–46 (Nos. 5500-5549) after mid-1946. The nose taper on the production models was already less pronounced than the prototypes', and its clean lines were interrupted by marker light/numberboard fairings moved from the upper boiler. Among the most obvious changes, cylinder skirts were removed, the original bulky pilot enclosure was slimmed and placed between the diagonal front portion of the running board skirts, and a lower headlight was added. Otto's distinctive portholes disappeared as well.

The T-1s gave yeoman's service during the early postwar years, handling all manner of Pennsy passenger trains. Despite a reputation as being slippery, their speed and performance was widely admired, and respected, by the men who ran them.

The Pennsy's aggressive postwar dieselization meant that America's largest fleet of streamlined steam locomotives was also among the shortest-lived. All T-1s

had been removed from service by 1952, and all were promptly scrapped.

Class Q-1 No. 6130 was a 4-6-4-4 duplex built as a prototype in 1942. Its "backward" rear cylinders invited damage and dirt—a design flaw avoided on the T-1—and its 77-inch drivers were too big

K-4s No. 5338 as shrouded, and as modified by 1947. TOP, H. K. VOLLRATH; ABOVE, JOE SCHMITZ COLL'N

PRR Q-1 No. 6130 at Mounds, Ohio, in 1944. BOB LORENZ

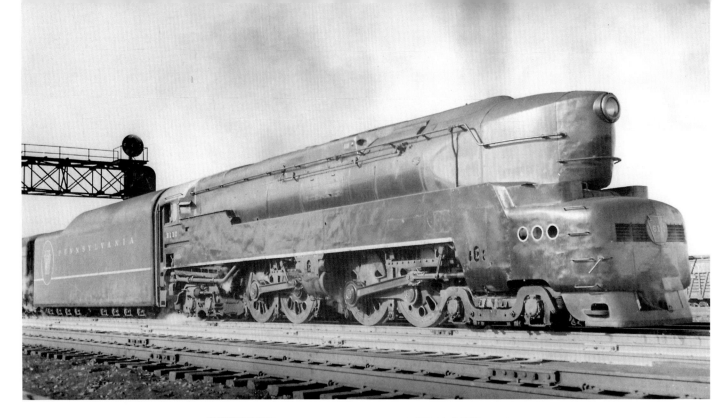

ABOVE: A collaboration between Baldwin Locomotive Works—long interested in developing duplex drives—and the PRR, T-1 prototypes Nos. 6110 and 6111 were delivered in April and May 1942. The duplex drive system reduced piston size and stroke, and cut the weight of reciprocating parts tied to a given set of cylinders, thereby reducing dynamic augment (the "pounding" inflicted on the track structure by the machinery's motion). Much of the T-1s' distinctive styling was the work of C. Louis Otto, an associate of Raymond Loewy. The two prototypes were delivered with long, tapered prows, portholed pilot enclosures, and deep skirts, as exemplified by No. 6110 on the *Trail Blazer* at Englewood, Ill., in January 1943.

MIDDLE: By the time of this December 3, 1949, view at East St. Louis, Ill., No. 6110 has been shorn of its deep skirts, and has had its pilot enclosure modified.

RIGHT: No. 6110 leads a mail and express train toward the MacArthur Bridge and St. Louis, circa 1944. The T-1s were designed to to operate over all PRR main lines, and could maintain schedules single-handedly in circumstances that formerly required the doubleheading of K-4s Pacifics.
ALL, J. R. QUINN COLLECTION

to provide the adhesion required in freight work. A conical smokebox front was marred by a traditionally bolted access door and a high-mounted headlight, but the locomotive's shrouded pilot, running board skirts, boiler jacket, cab, and tender were every bit as sleek as the T-1 prototypes'. By the time the Q-1's shortcomings had been addressed and corrected in 25 production Q-2 locomotives, the niceties of streamlining freight power were deemed largely unnecessary.

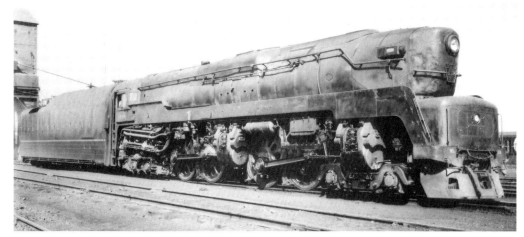

LEFT: The building of 50 production T-1s was divided between the PRR's Altoona Works (Nos. 5500-5524, in 1945) and Baldwin (Nos. 5525-5549, in 1946). They resembled the two prototypes of 1942, but stubbier prows and shallower running board skirts were the obvious cosmetic differences. No. 5501 displayed its as-built configuration at Englewood on May 26, 1946.

MIDDLE: Beginning in the summer of 1946, all T-1s had their cylinder skirts removed, running board steps added, and their pilot shrouds modified to the resultant narrower configuration visible on No. 5504 at East St. Louis in April 1948. The distinctive PRR keystone number boards were moved up to a new location on the prow, below the headlight.

BELOW: No. 5539 waited to lead an eastbound train from St. Louis Union Station on October 4, 1946. Built for speed, the T-1s routinely reached 100 MPH with heavy trains on long, straight sections of PRR main line, and were reported to have attained more than 130 MPH on rare occasions. Tenders were equipped with retractable scoops to take water "on the fly."
ALL, J. R. QUINN COLLECTION

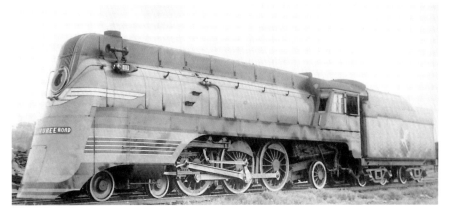

TOP: When F-1 Pacific No. 152 was photographed on the *Chippewa* at Milwaukee on October 4, 1951, only four other Milwaukee Road streamlined steam locomotives remained in service—Class A's Nos. 1 and 2, Class G No. 11, and sister F-1 No. 151. No. 152 went on to become the last active survivor until its December 1954 retirement. J. R. QUINN COLLECTION

ABOVE: Recently outshopped in its Kuhler-inspired shroud, No. 801 rested between *Midwest Hiawatha* connection assignments at Sioux Falls, S.D., in July 1941. HAROLD K. VOLLRATH COLLECTION

MIDWEST MODERNIZATION

The Milwaukee Road shrouded four vintage Pacifics—assigned to secondary service—to emulate the F-7 Hudsons.

Nos. 801 and 812 (the former Nos. 1523 and 1542) got makeovers and a new F-2 classification in 1941 to lead the *Midwest Hiawatha*, a train established on December 7, 1940. The main Chicago–Omaha stem of the train was powered by the Class A Atlantics of 1935, which had been displaced from the Chicago–Twin Cities *Hiawathas* by the recently delivered F-7 Hudsons. The two shrouded Class F-5 Pacifics forwarded a connecting section of the *Midwest Hiawatha* on its Manilla (Ia.)–Sioux Falls (S.D.) run. Electro-Motive E7 diesels became regular power on the train by 1948, and the two Pacifics were reassigned—a fate shared all too soon by the rest of the Milwaukee's steamliners.

Pacifics Nos. 151 and 152 were revamped and designated Class F-1 for

Chippewa service in 1941. No 152 was the original "protection" engine for the first *Hiawatha's* Class A Atlantics. Numbered 6160 and classed F-3cs at the time, the 1910-vintage Pacific was fitted with an oil tender and painted orange, maroon, and gray to match the *Hiawatha*.

It reverted to coal fuel in 1937 for assignment to the *Chippewa*, and retained its special paint. Renumbered 152 in 1939, the engine joined No. 151 at Milwaukee shops for shrouding two years later. In mid-1941, they replaced similarly painted but unshrouded F-3 Pacifics Nos. 177 (ex-6139) and 197 (ex-6168) on the *Chippewa*, and led the train's varied consist of heavyweight and lightweights cars between Milwaukee and Iron Mountain (Mich.)—later extended to Ontonagon, in Michigan's far Upper Peninsula. The train was re-equipped—even including re-assigned beaver-tail observation cars—and renamed the *Chippewa-Hiawatha* in the summer of 1948.

The streamlined F-1 Pacifics were replaced by diesels on the *Chippewa-Hiawatha* late in 1950. The pair outlived all other streamlined Milwaukee Road steam locomotives, with No. 152 earning the dubious honor of being the last Milwaukee Road steamliner retired, in December 1954.

During 1949, the Milwaukee Road also employed unstreamlined Class F-6 Hudsons and S-3 Northerns for a brief season in Idaho on the *Olympian Hiawatha* and *Columbian*.

The C&NW shrouded two Pacifics of its own in 1941. ES-class Nos. 1617 and 1620 were painted to blend with the road's new streamlined *"400"* lightweight cars.

Built in 1917, the Pacifics donned wide skirts, tall skyline casings, and narrow shovel noses to lead the *Minnesota 400* between Mankato (Minn.) and Wyeville (Wis.). Dark green on the skyline casing and upper boiler spilled down the nose in a deep "V" and continued back across the upper portions of cab and tender. Lower sheet metal was yellow with black pinstriping, all of which blended perfectly with the smoothsided Pullman-Standard rolling stock.

Migrating to other *"400"* connections over their careers, the pair became Nos. 617 and 620 in 1952, and were retired and scrapped four years later.

GOLDEN STATE GLORY

Picking up where the *Sunbeam* had left off, Southern Pacific tried its hand at some more in-house streamlining in 1941 with a group of P-10 Pacifics. These engines were given bullet noses, skyline casings, skirts, and paint to approximate the GS-class *Daylight* locomotives.

For its part, Lima continued to turn out genuine GS-class 4-8-4s: Nos. 4430-4449 were classed GS-4 and delivered in

1941; Nos. 4450-4457 arrived in 1942, also in class GS-4; and 1942 warbabies Nos. 4458 and 4459 were given their own GS-5 class by virtue of having roller bearings applied to all axles. Class GS-6 Nos. 4460-4469, delivered in 1943, were the last GS engines—with the abbreviation by then standing for General Service. This final group was equipped with 73.5-inch drivers, and reverted to the single headlight and non-vestibule cabs of the GS-3 and earlier variants. The GS-6 engines were

Chicago & North Western streamlined a pair of Pacifics in 1941 for *Minnesota 400* service. C&NW PHOTO; TLC COLLECTION

SP No. 4464 was one of ten GS-6s built by Lima in 1943 with the driver and cylinder dimensions of the GS-2s. Black paint and lack of skirting reflected the war effort. No. 4464 was at Mojave, Cal., in May 1949 on Train No. 51, the *San Joaquin/Sacramento Daylight*. J. R. QUINN COLLECTION

With Southern Pacific's GS-4 class came a revised smokebox door housing two lights—a Pyle Gyralite above and the standard fixed headlight below. Vestibule-type cabs also appeared on the GS-4s. This 1952 lineup at San Francisco included GS-2 No. 4411 and GS-4s 4454 and 4442.
C. THOMSON; JOE SCHMITZ COLLECTION

ABOVE: MT-4 Mountain No. 4352 and a mate led Train No. 51 at Woodford, California, in July 1946. Several members of this class were given skyline casings and *Daylight* paint on their tenders.

ABOVE RIGHT: P-10 Pacific No. 2484, among several streamstyled in 1941, had lost its *Daylight* colors by the time of this 1950 view at San Francisco.
BOTH, J. R. QUINN COLLECTION

RIGHT: The War Production Board authorized the diversion to Western Pacific of six GS-6 engines being built by Lima for Southern Pacific. WP GS-64 No. 484 paused with a passenger train at Salt Lake City on July 19, 1946. R. H. KENNEDY; JAY WILLIAMS COLLECTION

delivered without running board skirts in deference to wartime steel conservation, and wore utilitarian black paint.

Strapped for power during the war, Western Pacific prevailed upon the War Production Board in 1943 to divert six GS-6 locomotives from the SP order then under construction. Numbered 481-486

and classed GS-64 by WP, the locomotives' relatively clean lines were compromised for a time by the installation of "elephant ear" smoke lifters.

Southern Pacific's GS-class 4-8-4s could be seen throughout the SP system on trains like the *Cascade*, the *Lark*, the *Starlight*, the *Argonaut*, the *Sunset Limited*, and the *West Coast*, in addition to the *Daylights*. The big-windowed *Shasta Daylight* of 1949 was the first member of that illustrious fleet to be dieselized at its inception, and EMD E-units also took over the *Sunset Limited* when that train was re-equipped by Budd in 1950. For the GS-class, system-wide symbolism could be gleaned from the *Sunset's* name. The guard was changing.

Two GS-class locomotives avoided the scrapper, with GS-6 No. 4460 becoming a museum piece in St. Louis. GS-4 No. 4449, consigned to retirement display in a Portland, Oregon, park, was resurrected and restored to operation as part of the United States' bicentennial celebration. In patriotic red, white, and blue, the locomotive led the *American Freedom Train* in its travels beyond the tight-clearance Northeast. Kept in operation by volunteers and subsequently restored to a variety of paint schemes—notably its original *Daylight* colors—the big Northern remains active.

THE TENNESSEAN

Otto Kuhler's final steam "speedlining" commission was his personal favorite, and one for which he sought no payment.

The Southern Railway inaugurated a pair of stainless-sheathed P-S streamliners on the eve of the Second World War: the New Orleans–New York *Southerner*, and the Memphis–New York *Tennessean*. The latter was the re-equipped and renamed *Memphis Special*. Both trains were handled by the Pennsylvania Railroad between Washington Union Station and New York, and the *Tennessean* was operated in conjunction with the Norfolk & Western. N&W handled the train between Bristol (Tenn.) and Monroe (Va.). Balking at Southern's desire to employ run-through diesel power, steam stalwart N&W instead assigned one of its new Class J 4-8-4s to its 210-mile portion of the *Tennessean's* run.

Back on home rails for the 552 miles west of Bristol, Southern called the shots and moved the *Tennessean* to and from Memphis behind diesels. For the 165-mile leg over Southern rails from Washington to Monroe, however, steam proved to be a more cost-effective option even in the face of Southern's progressing dieselization.

Ps-4 Pacific No. 1380, built by Alco in 1923, was in Southern's Spencer (N.C.) shops at the time the *Tennessean's* motive power needs were being defined, and the 4-6-2 was selected to be streamlined to lead the new train between Monroe (near Lynchburg) and the nation's capital.

Southern's big Ps-4 Pacifics were already renowned for their elegant green paint, and Kuhler retained this hallmark in his "speedlining" of No. 1380.

The designer reached back to his *Royal Blue* commission of 1937 for some of his inspiration—No. 1380's smokebox shroud emulated the B&O Pacific's torpedo nose cone right down to the concentric trim circles around the centered headlight. The full-length skyline casing ended in a smoothly beveled air intake trimmed with stainless steel. A few feet behind this, the casing widened to incorporate marker light and numberboard housings. This combination of smokebox and skyline was a dead ringer for one of Kuhler's mid-1930s conceptual drawings published in Robert Henry's 1937 *Portraits of the Iron Horse*. The gap between the smooth pilot and the nose cone was bridged by a thick fin, another Kuhler trademark.

Southern's only streamlined locomotive, Ps-4 No. 1380, was styled by Otto Kuhler to pull the Washington, DC–Monroe, Va. segment of the *Tennessean*. Bumped by diesels after the war, the green-and-silver engine found work elsewhere on the Southern system, and in this view leads Train No. 135 north of Atlanta. L. A. MCLEAN; TLC COLLECTION

Narrow running board skirts curved down around the cylinders and were trimmed in a sweeping crescent—a subtle bid on Kuhler's part, perhaps, for consideration when the time came to streamline Southern's flagship *Crescent Limited.* (Not fully re-equipped until 1950, Southern's fleet leader debuted its new P-S and Budd cars behind diesels.)

A Southern Railway medallion on each cylinder cover, polished cylinder head covers, and gold-tone trim enhanced the streamlined package. The *Tennessean's* name was discretely lettered on the stainless steel running board skirt above the first driver. The metallic stripe continued back across the cab and—in aluminum paint—onto the tender. The tender sides were bisected by a curving diagonal separation between the engine's green paint and an aluminum-painted aft portion designed to blend with the stainless-sheathed cars.

A total of 26 cars arrived from P-S in 1941 for the new *Tennessean,* in baggage-mail, baggage-dormitory-coach, full coach, divided ("Jim Crow") coach, diner, and tavern-lounge-observation floor plans. All cars were named for on-line communities.

Free to continue its aggressive dieselization after the war, Southern repowered its Washington Division trains and demoted No. 1380 and its unstreamlined Ps-4 rostermates to general duties.

Kuhler's streamlined steam swan song was officially retired on July 29, 1953, and scrapped.

Among his many streamlined steam commissions, Otto Kuhler regarded Southern No. 1380 as his favorite. It was also his last. BELOW, TLC COLLECTION; BELOW RIGHT, BOB'S PHOTOS COLLECTION

BOTTOM: No. 1380 leads the ten-car Pullman-Standard *Tennessean* south through Alexandria, Va., and past the George Washington Masonic Memorial in 1941. WILEY BRYAN; TLC PUBLISHING COLLECTION

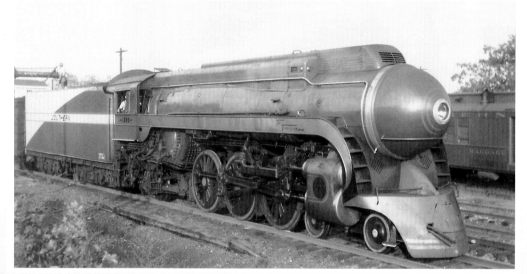

FIRST OF THE LAST

Norfolk & Western, a steam stalwart by virtue of its strong ties to the Appalachian coal industry, was also in the vanguard of steam locomotive design and construction. The N&W's Roanoke (Va.) shops, renowned for its innovation and precision, turned out a fleet of 14 Class J 4-8-4s between 1941 and 1950.

Nos. 600-604, delivered between October 1941 and January 1942, introduced the Js' torpedo styling. The work of F. C. Noel, an N&W tool designer, this treatment conveyed both sleekness and power. A hemispherical nose topped a smooth pilot, with a sculpted skyline cas-

ing flowing back into the cab roofline. Running board skirts—not too wide—curved up from the pilot beam and formed a Tuscan-red stripe that contrasted with the overall black engine and was carried through the cab and across the huge tender. Minimal gold lettering—road number on the skirt and road name on the tender—was placed within the red stripe. Cylinders and running gear were left entirely accessible, although firebox sides were skirted.

One of the challenges facing N&W's Roanoke design team, led by C. H. Harris and G. P. McGavock, was to develop a locomotive able to speed over the water-

Norfolk & Western's Class J 4-8-4 debuted in 1941. Delivery of the final examples by the N&W's Roanoke shops in 1950 brought down the curtain on streamlined steam production in North America. N&W PHOTO; TLC PUBLISHING COLLECTION

No. 607, leading the *Powhatan Arrow* at Kenova, W. Va., in July 1947, was one of six J's built by N&W during the war without streamlining and designated Class J1. They were shrouded after the war to match Nos. 600-604. J. R. QUINN COLLECTION

No. 605, another warbaby, pauses at Roanoke with the westbound *Tennessean* in April 1957. J. R. QUINN COLLECTION

With a heavyweight diner in its otherwise streamlined consist, the *Powhatan Arrow* follows the New River near Eggleston, Virginia, in 1947. N&W PHOTO

level grades at the east and west ends of the railroad without incurring a performance penalty through the N&W's mountainous heart. Drivers of 70-inch diameter were chosen in deference to this variable profile and made the engines look even bigger than they were.

Nos. 600-604 established the mechanical and performance parameters

for the class, although the first 11 engines' 275-PSI boiler pressure was raised to the 300-PSI design pressure to match later Nos. 611-613. Engine weight was 494,000 pounds. Tractive force of Nos. 600-610 was a mighty 73,300 pounds—this was increased to a phenomenal 80,000 pounds in the final three Js, greater than any other 4-8-4. Remarkably, No. 604 was even briefly fitted with a trailing-truck booster that added another 5,500 pounds of tractive force.

The J's were capable of achieving, and sometimes exceeding, 90 MPH with as many as 15 cars in tow, and were unfazed by N&W's mainline grades of as much as 2.0%. Normal top speed was 80 MPH, but the officially recorded maximum was 110 MPH with 15 cars on a straight, level run. Roller bearings were employed throughout, and extensive use was made of mechanical lubrication.

Twelve-wheeled tenders held 35 tons of coal and 20,000 gallons of water, contributing to a reduction in en-route servicing that further aided time-keeping.

The next batch of N&W 4-8-4s was built during the war, in 1943, as Class J1. Nos. 605-610 did without their predecessors' streamlining until material restric-

tions eased after V-J Day and they were retrofitted. The final three J's, Nos. 611-613, emerged from Roanoke in 1950. They proved to be the last 4-8-4s, and the last streamlined steam locomotives, built in North America.

Between 1945 and 1947, 22 USRA-designed Heavy 4-8-2s were put through a modernization program at Roanoke that included high-capacity tenders and shrouds matching the Class Js'. Class K-2 Nos. 116-125 had been built by Alco in 1919, and K-2a Nos. 126-137 were delivered by Baldwin in 1923. The K-2 and K-2a's were denizens of the N&W's Shenandoah Valley line where they led, among others, trains carrying through cars between Roanoke and New York City.

Streamlining on the N&W had been extended beyond locomotives to passenger cars in 1941 with the acquisition of Pullman-Standard coaches 1720-1734, and by the presence of the stainless-sheathed *Tennessean* operated in conjunction with the Southern Railway.

N&W entered the postwar streamliner spotlight by refurbishing its 1941 P-S coaches as the core of the brand-new *Powhatan Arrow*, which made its first run on April 28, 1946. The daytime consist was dressed in the same subdued Tuscan red livery worn by N&W's heavyweight cars. The *Powhatan Arrow's* schedule required just under 16 hours for the 676.6-mile Norfolk–Cincinnati journey.

The 1946 consist was merely a stop-gap until N&W could take delivery of brand-new streamlined equipment ordered that same year. A steel strike, national labor unrest, component shortages, and pent-up demand from the war years had created huge backlogs with the commercial passenger carbuilders as railroads across the country sought to re-equip their exhausted fleets. Delivery schedules of as long as four years prompted many roads, like N&W, to make interim arrangements until Pullman-Standard, Budd, and the other builders could deliver.

P-S finally came through for N&W in November 1949—more than three years after the order had been placed—with two all-new *Powhatan Arrow* consists complete with dining and round-ended observation cars.

The older streamlined coaches were reassigned to overnight running mates like the *Pocahontas* and *Cavalier*, which

would benefit from partial re-equipping with new lightweight Budd 10-6 sleeping cars in 1950.

The J's and modernized K-2 and K-2a's retained their place at the head of N&W's premier passenger trains until the summer of 1958, when leased RF&P E8s dieselized the N&W's varnish and briefly bumped the J's to freight service.

Class J No. 611 survived scrapping, first as a Roanoke museum piece following donation by N&W in 1959 and then, after a 1982–83 restoration, as an operating ambassador for N&W corporate successor Norfolk Southern. In 1984 the American Society of Mechanical Engineers (ASME) declared the locomotive a National Historic Engineering Landmark. Its second career in excursion service at an end, No. 611 returned to museum display in Roanoke in 1996.

Class J No. 603 was paced leading an eastbound passenger train through West Virginia in 1953. ROBERT HALE; JAY WILLIAMS COLLECTION

Look closely—that's not a J coming off the Shenandoah Valley line at Roanoke in this mid-1950s scene, but rather K-2a No. 130, one of 22 heavy Pacifics modernized by N&W at Roanoke after the war and shrouded in imitation of the J's. JAY WILLIAMS COLLECTION

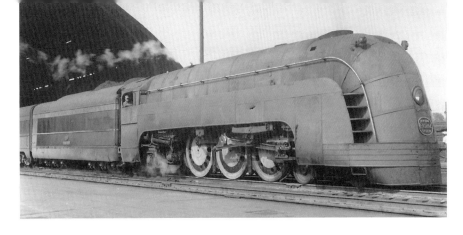

Bumped from the *Mercury*, NYC No. 4915 led the *James Whitcomb Riley* on the IC at Chicago in 1942. No. 4917 was at Indianapolis in 1941. TOP, JAY WILLIAMS COLLECTION; ABOVE, TLC COLLECTION

The *Riley's* original observation car was a product of Beech Grove. The train, with P-S coaches, was near Aroma Park, Ill., in August 1945. JAY WILLIAMS COLLECTION

HOOSIER HAPPENINGS

New York Central's *Mercury* Pacifics were reassigned to their old "Big Four" territory—NYC's Cleveland, Cincinnati, Chicago & St. Louis Railroad subsidiary—in 1939 after being supplanted by streamlined Hudsons on the longer and heavier *Mercury* consists. Retaining their Dreyfuss shrouding, the Pacifics were repainted gray and red to match the consist of the

new Cincinnati–Indianapolis–Chicago *James Whitcomb Riley*, inaugurated on April 28, 1941. Named for the famous Hoosier poet, the *Riley* was an all-coach daylight schedule leaving Cincinnati Union Terminal in the morning, with an evening return from the Windy City's Illinois Central station.

"The *James Whitcomb Riley* is dedicated to de-luxe, low-cost economy coach travel for the 'home folk' and commercial travelers of America," stated NYC in the train's inaugural brochure.

The original seven-car consist, well within the Pacifics' capabilities, included three heavyweights—a baggage, diner, and observation modernized at Beech Grove—along with four new Budd coaches (Nos. 2560-2563). The entire train, including the fluted stainless steel cars, was styled by Dreyfuss and given a bright red window band, with gray bodies for the non-Budd cars. The *Riley's* name was lettered on the side of each Pacific's cab.

Heavy wartime traffic saw the Budd cars replaced by six similarly painted Pullman-Standard coaches (Nos. 2601-2606). Other consist adjustments were made right after the war, and in 1947 the Dreyfuss Pacifics were replaced by unstreamlined Hudsons Nos. 5333 and 5401.

A 1948 re-equipping brought more Budd cars to the *Riley*—this time in completely unpainted stainless steel—including a round-ended tavern-lounge-observation car.

TRAIN OF INFAMY

Capping off the exotic mix of steamliners debuting in 1941 was a pair of stainless steel consists delivered by Budd to New York Central. The cars were intended to re-equip the storied *Empire State Express* to mark its 50th birthday. The train operated on a daylight New York–Buffalo–Cleveland schedule, with a connection to Detroit from Buffalo via NYC's Canada Southern mainline route.

A total of 26 cars was delivered, divided among six floor plans: two baggage-mail; two baggage-tavern-lounge; six parlor; four diner; ten coach; and two tavern-lounge-observation. All were named in honor of New York State governors, with the two most distinguished names—*Theodore Roosevelt* and *Franklin D. Roosevelt*—reserved for the round-ended observation cars.

To power the two consists, NYC clad J-3a Hudsons Nos. 5426 and 5429 in a striking hybrid version of Dreyfuss' 1938 *20th Century Limited* streamlining.

The hemispherical smokebox cover was there, *sans* vertical crest but with a larger-diameter lower half. The skyline casing extended forward from the cab to a pillbox-like terminus ahead of the stack. Shrouding below the rounded nose generally mirrored that on the earlier ten Hudsons. The upper half of the nose and boiler jacket was painted aluminum, with the skyline casing and all sheet metal below the demarcation gloss black. What really set these two Hudsons apart, though, was the application of Budd stainless steel fluting panels to the engine skirting and tender. Wide flutes were placed below the rear portion of the running board and cab. The tender was stratified to match the car exteriors, with alternating narrow-flute, wide-flute, blank, and narrow-flute panels extending up the sides. Cast-metal representations of the train name and NYC oval medallion graced the shroud above the pilot. Cab and tender lettering were black.

The *Empire State Express* on a pre-inaugural run at Cold Spring, N.Y.
NYC PHOTO; TLC PUBLISHING COLLECTION

An early *Empire State* brochure.
AUTHOR'S COLLECTION

BACK TO THE DRAWING BOARD

Baltimore & Ohio's streamlined *Cincinnatian* debuted on January 19, 1947, as a 12.5-hour Baltimore–Cincinnati daylight coach schedule intended, in part, to pre-empt looming—but ultimately unfulfilled—competition from Chesapeake & Ohio.

A pair of five-car *Cincinnatian* consists was created in 1946 at the B&O's Mount Clare (Baltimore) shops. Built atop the six-wheel-trucked underframes of existing heavyweights, the *Cincinnatian's* cars emerged with extensively welded bodies, streamlined roof contours, and full-width diaphragms. Each consist offered a baggage-buffet-lounge car, three coaches, and a round-ended diner-lounge-observation car. Their six-wheel trucks gave away the secret to informed observers, but Mount Clare had worked a marvelous transformation. B&O had been able to join the postwar streamliner frenzy near its peak, without the expense and delays of dealing with the commercial car builders. Mount Clare's skills were honed in the late 1930s, when the shops turned out similar—but not nearly as sleek—modernized heavyweight consists for the B&O's diesel-powered *Capitol Limited* and *National Limited.*

To B&O Research Engineer Olive W. Dennis goes the credit for designing the streamlining applied to four 20-year-old Baldwin Pacifics (Nos. 5301-5304) assigned to the new *Cincinnatians.* Dennis was the first female civil engineer hired by a U.S. railroad (in 1921), and her early responsibilities as Engineer of Service shaped the presentation of B&O passenger service for many years. Among her most noteworthy contributions in this regard were designs for B&O's famous "Blue" dining car china, introduced in 1927 for the railroad's centennial.

On her *Cincinnatian* Pacifics, Dennis merged a broad, rounded nose into a generous boiler jacket, topped with a squat full-length skyline. Square-edged skirting slanted up at a 30-degree angle from the pilot beam before edging the running board. The same angle was repeated in aluminum-framed black panels on the boiler, running board and firebox skirts, and tender. Even the cab window frames tilted back at 30 degrees. Cab gangways were left unenclosed, but a full-width diaphragm did conceal the gap between the tender and first car. The locomotives

Bumped by diesels, the *Empire State Express* Hudsons were reassigned to the Midwest after the war. No. 5429 sported a *Mercury* nameplate on the IC at Chicago. BOB'S PHOTOS COLLECTION

Another locomotive assigned to the post-1939 *Mercury* trains was the former *Commodore Vanderbilt,* No. 5344, reshrouded in 1939 to match the Dreyfuss Hudsons (one of which, No. 5445, also saw *Mercury* service). The former *Commodore Vanderbilt* led the *Mercury* east out of Chicago's Central Station in November 1939. H. H. HARWOOD COLLECTION; BROCHURE, AUTHOR'S COLLECTION

The re-equipped *Empire State Express* was a marvelously executed steamliner, and consolation of sorts for Budd's fruitless efforts to build equipment for the 1938 *20th Century Limited.* The gleam of the *Empire State Express,* however, was diminished by world events on the train's December 7, 1941, debut.

Before they lost their stainless shrouds in 1949–50, the two *Empire State Express* Hudsons could also be seen on trains like the *Mercury* and the Chicago–Detroit *Twilight Limited.*

the
MERCURY
CHICAGO • DETROIT
TOLEDO • CLEVELAND

NEW YORK CENTRAL SYSTEM

MT. CLARE EMPLOYEES OF B & O FOLLOWING MEETING, DEC. 31, 1946, WHEN PRESIDENT WHITE PRAISED THEIR EXCELLENT WORK ON "CINCINNATIAN"

were painted royal blue overall, with the aforementioned black and aluminum trim. Names of the train—in script—and the railroad appeared on the tender, while each locomotive's number was applied to the running board skirt amidships.

The Class P-7 4-6-2s underwent a thorough mechanical and structural upgrade in addition to the cosmetic improvements. The quartet received new cast frames with integral cylinders, feedwater heaters, relocated and shielded air pumps and centered headlights. These modifications, in concert with the cosmetic changes, resulted in the four being moved into their own P-7d class. Finally, they were mated with larger tenders to help them cope with the tough new schedule. Even with the overhaul, the Pacifics were limited to a five-car consist. Anything heavier would have required helper service over the Alleghenies, as a Class P-7d could just manage the *Cincinnatian* up and over Seventeen Mile Grade's 2.2% unassisted. Two of the Pacifics split each Baltimore–Cincinnati run, changing at Grafton, West Virginia.

B&O P-7d No. 5304 was notable as one of only two American steam locomotives to be streamlined twice, sharing the honor with NYC No. 5344, the *Commodore Vanderbilt* (facing page). Shorn of its *Royal Blue* Otto Kuhler styling in 1939 and temporarily reverting to its original P-7 class,

Former *Royal Blue* Pacific No. 5304 starred at the *Cincinnatian's* rollout. B&O PHOTO; TLC COLLECTION

No. 5304 leads the *Cincinnatian* on October 13, 1949. WILLIAM P. PRICE; TLC PUBLISHING COLLECTION

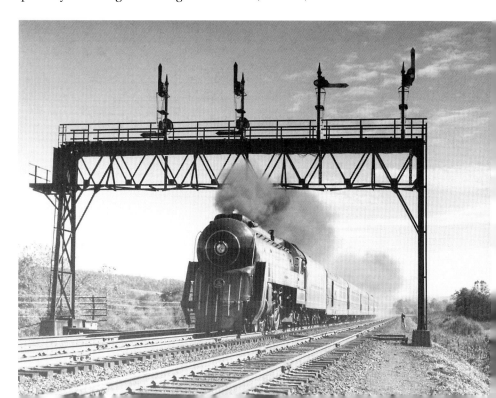

B&O No. 5304 emerged from Mount Clare with its three *Cincinnatian* mates in Dennis' brawnier torpedo styling.

When B&O management came to terms with what C&O Chairman Robert R. Young already knew—that no viable daylight market existed between Cincinnati and the nation's capital—the *Cincinnatian's* cars and P-7d Pacifics were shifted in mid-1950 to tap the more lucrative trade between Detroit and Cincinnati. Revenue on the equipment's new route was augmented by head-end mail and express, which could be accommodated in additional cars behind the P-7d's given the territory's flatter profile. EMD diesels took over the *Cincinnatian* in 1956—the year before Dennis' death—with the four streamlined Pacifics briefly reassigned to Louisville before retirement.

UPPER RIGHT: B&O P-7d No. 5302. B&O PHOTO; AUTHOR'S COLLECTION

RIGHT: After three years of disappointing traffic on its original Baltimore–Washington–Cincinnati route, the *Cincinnatian* equipment was shifted to a Detroit–Cincinnati schedule. This 1955 edition passing through Lima, Ohio, included a heavyweight RPO and coach. LOUIS A. MARRE COLLECTION

FACING PAGE, TOP: Floor plans of the *Cincinnatian's* baggage-buffet-lounge, 60-seat coach, and diner-observation cars. RAILWAY AGE

FACING PAGE, BOTTOM: The westbound *Cincinnatian*—with *Fountain Square* on the rear—passes the tower at Bond, Md., on October 12, 1949. WILLIAM P. PRICE; TLC COLLECTION

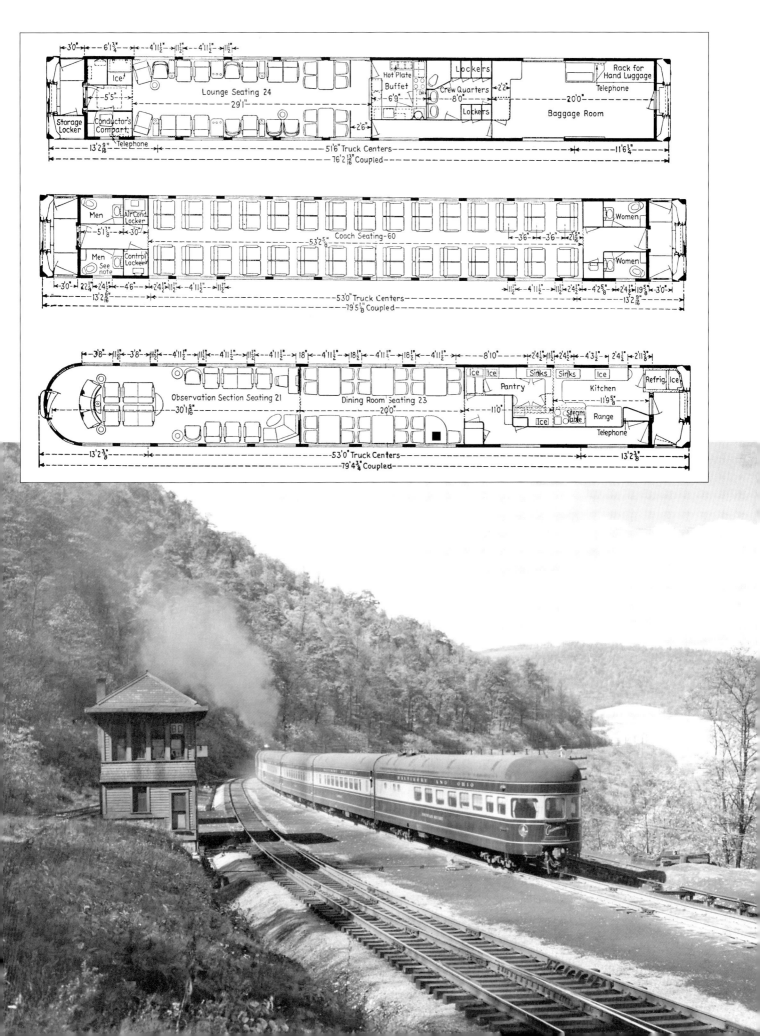

Lounge Seating 24 — 29'1"
Ice
Storage Locker
Conductor's Compart.
Telephone
13'2 9/16"
Hot Plate
Buffet — 6'9"
Crew Quarters — 8'0"
Lockers
2'2"
Rack for Hand Luggage
Telephone
Baggage Room — 20'0"
51'6" Truck Centers
11'6 1/4"
76'2 13/16" Coupled

Men
Air Cond. Locker
Men See note
Control Locker
Coach Seating-60 — 53'2 7/8"
Women
Women
13'2 9/16"
53'0" Truck Centers
79'5 11/16" Coupled
13'2 9/16"

Observation Section Seating 21 — 30'1 3/4"
Dining Room Seating 23 — 20'0"
Ice Ice
Pantry — 11'0"
Sinks Sinks Ice
Kitchen — 11'9 5/8"
Ice Steam Table Range
Telephone
Refrig. Ice
13'2 3/8"
53'0" Truck Centers
13'2 3/8"
79'4 3/4" Coupled

BALTIMORE AND OHIO

THE BANDWAGON

Many of the streamlined steam locomotives that burnished North American rails in regular service between 1934 and 1959 were the creations of leading industrial designers or talented railroad engineering departments.

Alas, some were not. In their zeal—or desperation—to jump on the streamlined bandwagon, a handful of railroads cobbled chrome and sheet metal onto an old steam locomotive or two and called it a day. Others tried harder, with mixed results. Despite their esthetic good intentions, these railroads produced locomotives ranging in appearance from awkward to simply odd.

For roads like Illinois Central, Frisco, Wabash, Texas & Pacific, and even little Rutland, wide running board skirts and perhaps some pilot sheeting were enough to draw attention to their attempts to bolster passenger or freight business.

Illinois Central gave 1916-vintage Pacific No. 1146 extra-wide running board skirts, a "chin" shroud, and revamped lettering in the late 1940s to lead the Fulton (Ky.)–Louisville connecting section of the new, streamlined Chicago–New Orleans *City of New Orleans*.

The Delaware, Lackawanna & Western gained notoriety in the late 1930s and 1940s for a gaggle of locomotives styled, as far as anyone knew, by Mother Goose herself. A profusion of wings and stylized feathers adorned modestly streamstyled Pacifics, Atlantics, Ten Wheelers, and Hudsons on "The Route of Phoebe Snow."

One of the Lackawanna's winged wonders, 4-6-2 No. 1123 poked out of Buffalo's Bush trainshed on June 13, 1937. JAY WILLIAMS COLLECTION

The closest Illinois Central came to operating a streamlined steam locomotive was Pacific No. 1146, dressed up after the war for service on a *City of New Orleans* connection. It was photographed at Fulton, Ky., in May 1949. HAROLD K. VOLLRATH COLLECTION

Lettered for service on the *Louisiana Eagle*, Texas & Pacific 4-6-2 No. 704 showed off its yellow and blue colors at New Orleans in October 1949. HAROLD K. VOLLRATH COLLECTION

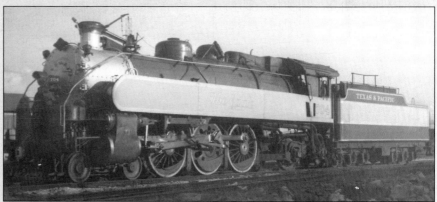

continued on page 130

UPPER LEFT AND ABOVE: Hans Christian Andersen would have appreciated this member of the Lackawanna's streamstyled flock. Atlantic No. 988 was transformed by the road's Scranton (Pa.) shops from "Camelback" to conventional cab configuration, and earned its wings in the process. Shown at Washington, N.J., in 1934 and 1947. BOTH, H. K. VOLLRATH COLLECTION

LEFT: Boston & Maine's P-4a Pacifics, 1934 Lima products, sported partial skyline casings, round-cornered cab fronts, and rakish tender lettering. No. 3710, *Peter Cooper*, was at Portland, Me., in 1942. JAY WILLIAMS COLLECTION

BELOW: Delaware & Hudson favored Anglicized lines, as on 4-6-2 No. 609 at Montreal circa 1940. CPR PHOTO; AUTHOR'S COLLECTION

The New York, Ontario & Western (NYO&W) enlisted Otto Kuhler in 1936 to restyle 4-8-2 Mountain No. 405 and a group of heavyweight coaches operating as the *Mountaineer*, aboard which residents of New York City and suburban New Jersey could escape to resorts in the nearby Catskill Mountains. Kuhler gave the *Mountaineer* a maroon and orange livery replete with Art Deco accents, but left the cars unstreamlined. The total effect—with skirted running boards on the engine and a pinstriped, multicolored livery trailing from tender to cars—foreshadowed the peripatetic designer's work on Lehigh Valley's *Asa Packer* two years later.

The six-car *Valley Flyer* was a seasonal Santa Fe train inaugurated on June 11, 1939, operating between Oakland and Bakersfield through California's San Joaquin Valley. Elderly Pacifics Nos. 1369 and 1376 were given wide running board skirts, some other bits of cosmetic sheeting, and a silver-sided paint scheme in 1939. The six trailing heavyweight cars were also painted silver, and shared the engines' red and yellow trim striping.

Another road to dress up steam power without resorting to full streamlining was Nashville, Chattanooga & St. Louis (NC&StL), applying conical noses to a group of 4-8-4s and yellow-striped running boards and tenders to several more.

Toledo, Peoria & Western adopted similar running board striping on 4-8-4s, as did Minneapolis & St. Louis on 4-6-2 No. 502 and several 2-8-2s. Southern dressed up Ps-2 Pacific No. 6470 with a conical nose, but like most it was a poor substitute for the fully streamlined creations of Kuhler, Dreyfuss, and Loewy.

The New York, Ontario & Western's seasonal *Mountaineer* made it possible for New Yorkers to escape to the Catskills. Otto Kuhler relied mostly on paint to spruce up 4-8-2 No. 405 and its heavyweight consist. TLC PUBLISHING COLLECTION

Santa Fe's *Valley Flyer* was another seasonal train comprising heavyweight cars and snappily painted, but unstreamlined, power. HAROLD K. VOLLRATH COLLECTION

Frisco applied wide running board skirts and prominent identification to a number of Hudsons, Mountains, and Pacifics beginning in the late 1930s. J. R. QUINN COLLECTION

LATE FOR THE PARTY

Robert R. Young, enigmatic postwar chairman of the Chesapeake & Ohio, opted to provide two connecting services for his Washington–Cincinnati *Chessie*, the Budd-built daytime domeliner destined never to turn a revenue mile. Overseeing a blue-chip coal-hauler, Young made the prudent decision to power his new streamliner with steam—unproven turbine-electrics for the mainline trunk and rebuilt heavy Pacifics for the Newport News (Va.) and Louisville branches.

The C&O went to town with these modernized locomotives. A quintet of F-19 Pacifics entered the C&O's Huntington (W. Va.) shops in 1946 for conversion to L-1 Hudsons. The first one outshopped, No. 494, emerged in conventional, if hulking, steam locomotive silhouette. The remaining four, Nos. 490-493, were given orange-and-stainless steel shrouds to match the trailing Budd cars.

Streamlining also had been proposed for Class J-3a 4-8-4 "Greenbriers" Nos. 610-614 of 1948 but was cancelled to cut costs after construction had begun at Lima. Smooth pilots were a vestige of the Greenbriers' aborted streamlining. Earlier renderings of a proposed but never-built streamlined C&O *George Washington* consist depicted a shrouded 4-8-4 clearly inspired by the same Ohio builder's Southern Pacific *Daylight* locomotives.

Unfortunately for the L-1 Hudsons, the train they were built to haul died at birth in one of the most puzzling about-faces in postwar railroading. Years of advertising build-up and pre-inaugural equipment display tours notwithstanding, C&O management after 1948 behaved as if the *Chessie* had never existed. Most of the Budd cars were sold, and three huge steam-turbine-electric locomotives built to pull the mainline *Chessie* were returned to the builder and scrapped. Although they never pulled their intended charge in revenue service,

the streamlined Hudsons—dubbed "Yellowbellies" by crews—earned their keep for several years hauling other mainline schedules across C&O's map. In 1950, with most of C&O's truncated 1946 order of P-S stainless-sheathed lightweight cars finally delivered, L-1 No. 490 was dispatched with a touring exhibition consist.

No. 490 also led the last C&O steam-powered passenger train, on June 7, 1953. Streamlining intact, the L-1 survives as a static exhibit at Baltimore's B&O Museum.

The C&O's trio of M-1 steam-turbine-electrics, unlike N&W's subsequent and outwardly similar *Jawn Henry*, was designed and built specifically for passenger service. They traced their lineage back to an oil-burning demonstrator built by

There was a bit of Dreyfuss Hudson and Reading *Crusader* in the treatment of Chesapeake & Ohio's four streamlined L-1 Hudsons of 1947. The stainless steel fin above the headlight evoked the same Spartan helmet comparison brought to mind by Dreyfuss' NYC design of 1938. Beyond that, however, the C&O quartet broke new ground, with their forward-thrusting front ends that merged elements of shovel-nose and torpedo styling. C&O PHOTO; C&OHS COLLECTION

Plans to streamline a group of five C&O 4-8-4 Greenbriers were shelved, but this rendering hints at what might have been. C&O; C&OHS COLLECTION

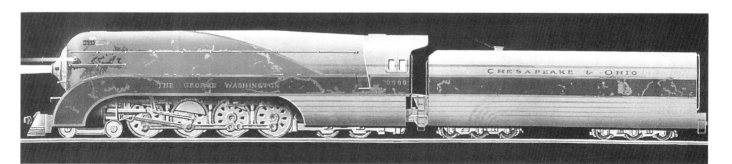

Like bees on a bright orange flower, workers at the C&O's Huntington, W. Va., shops put the finishing touches on rebuilt and streamlined L-1 Hudson No. 490 in early 1947. This was the first L-1 to be shrouded, although No. 494 was outshopped before it.
C&O PHOTO; C&OHS COLLECTION

No. 494—at Washington's Ivy City terminal in July 1952—was every bit an L-1 from a mechanical perspective, but was never shrouded. The entire class was rebuilt from F-19 Pacifics.
C&O PHOTO; C&OHS COLLECTION

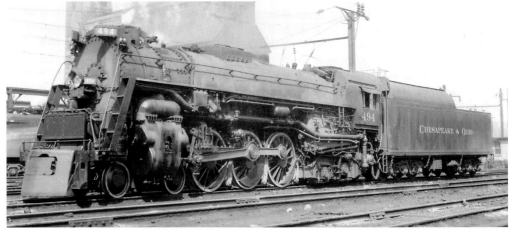

C&O L-1 No. 492, also at Ivy City, affords a "before-and-after" comparison with unstreamlined but similarly rebuilt No. 494. Note the larger C&O "donut" insignia, and the addition of an illuminated numberbox above the pilot. Five L-2 Hudsons built by Baldwin in 1948 were to have been shrouded but, like the J-3a Greenbrier 4-8-4s delivered the same year by Lima, streamlining was omitted to cut costs. C&O PHOTO;
C&OHS COLLECTION

General Electric in 1938 for the Union Pacific and later sampled by Great Northern before being scrapped in 1944.

Other turbine developments followed. Baldwin and Westinghouse collaborated on an experimental steam turbine for the PRR in 1944, a 6-8-6 wheel arrangement Class S-2 numbered 6800 and employing a geared, rather than electrical, drive. Pennsy followed up with a January 1945 proposal for a "Triplex" turbine, styled by Raymond Loewy Associates, that never left the drawing board.

Determined to procure innovative coal-burning locomotives for his *Chessie*, Young authorized an order for three M-1 turbines from Baldwin-Westinghouse in the fall of 1946—the builders had been developing such a project since 1945, and the C&O was the perfect "showcase" customer. The orange-and-gray behemoths were 145 feet long and weighed nearly 1.25 million pounds—on both counts, the largest steam locomotives ever. Riding on a 4-8-4-8-4 wheel arrangement, the units' powerplant components were concealed within a streamlined carbody. Inside the nose, ahead of the cab, was the 29-ton coal bunker, covered by a pair of doors to minimize airborne dust. Behind the cab was a conventional firebox and boiler, but oriented "backwards" with the firebox leading. The turbine and generator assembly—converting steam to electricity to power the traction motors—was immediately aft of the smokebox. A separate tender, contoured to resemble the *Chessie's* Budd equipment, toted 25,000 gallons of water.

No. 500 arrived on the C&O in June 1947, and Nos. 501 and 502 followed in mid-1948. Even with the *Chessie's* cancel-

Brand-new Baldwin-Westinghouse M-1 steam-turbine-electric No. 500 was on display to the industry at Atlantic City, N.J., on June 22, 1947. The handrails and numberboard/marker light assemblies on the unit's nose were subsequently modified.
H. REID; C&OHS COLLECTION

lation, the M-1s spent nearly two years in revenue service between Charlottesville (Va.) and Cincinnati. Ongoing steam pressure problems and other teething bugs—along with the promise of a substantial refund—convinced the C&O to return the trio to the builders in 1949.

THE CITY OF MEMPHIS

The Nashville, Chattanooga & St. Louis (NC&StL) inaugurated America's last stem-to-stern steamliner on May 17, 1947, with its homebuilt, six-car Nashville–Memphis *City of Memphis*.

With a budget of $350,000, Superintendent of Machinery C. M. Darden and his West Nashville shop forces turned a half-dozen veteran Pullman parlor cars into blue-and-silver streamliners, powered by a 34-year-old Pacific given a "bathtub" shroud and mechanical upgrades for the occasion. This final American design for a streamlined steam locomotive was not far removed from the first—in silhouette, NC&StL Class K-2d

Pacific No. 535 evoked the shovel-nosed "bathtub" shroud of NYC's *Commodore Vanderbilt*. The "Dixie Line" 4-6-2 received new cylinders and frame components along with roller bearings on all engine and tender axles. The 12-wheel tender held enough coal and water—16 tons and 15,000 gallons—to eliminate all but one service stop on the *City of Memphis'* route.

The 194-seat consist included a baggage-mail car, three coaches, a diner, and a pug-ended lounge-observation car. Ridership was so strong that standees were

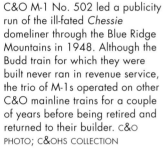

C&O M-1 No. 502 led a publicity run of the ill-fated *Chessie* domeliner through the Blue Ridge Mountains in 1948. Although the Budd train for which they were built never ran in revenue service, the trio of M-1s operated on other C&O mainline trains for a couple of years before being retired and returned to their builder. C&O PHOTO; C&OHS COLLECTION

occasionally seen, and extra coaches—some of which were eventually streamlined to match—were frequently added on weekends and holidays.

Even with its new looks, No. 535's age caught up with it. Barely two years after the train's debut, the scheduled five hours over a demanding 239-mile route had taken a sufficient toll that the streamlined Pacific was withdrawn from *City of Memphis* service and replaced by one of the Dixie Line's 4-8-4s.

GRAY GHOST

The Richmond, Fredericksburg & Potomac's sole entry into the steamliner parade lasted a scant four months.

The *Old Dominion* was inaugurated by the RF&P on November 16, 1947, as a day train between Washington, DC, and Richmond, Virginia. A pinstriped gray consist of five lightweight ACF cars included four 70-seat coaches and parlor-diner *Virginia Dare*. The plan was to make two daily round-trips, pulled by unstreamlined steam locomotives, over the 113.5-mile route, but the *Old Dominion* was absent from the RF&P timetable by March 1948.

DIESELS AND DENOUEMENT

In the 1940s, railroads as powerful and influential as NYC, PRR, SP, N&W, and B&O had demonstrated that the streamlined form and the steam locomotive still had a prominent place in American railroading, pre- and postwar.

In a very real sense, it was the war, and the domestic progress and expectations it begat, that killed steam in America. Streamlined steam was still evolving—witness the most powerful 4-8-4's on the continent, built by N&W in

1950, in their sculpted skins—but got caught in the crossfire between diesel and status quo.

General Motors' FT road freight diesel had come of age during a war it helped win. GM's passenger diesels—no more sleek or colorful or seductive than many of their streamlined steam contemporaries—nonetheless had a foot firmly in the door before their manufacture was suspended by the War Production Board. The term "Diesel-Powered" had acquired a certain cachet, and was appearing in conjunction with more and more streamliner listings in the *Official Guide*. By the time EMD and its emerging competitors could resume production of their passenger diesels after the war, equipment-starved railroads were beating down the builders' doors with orders to placate an increasingly fickle public. Color was good. Streamlined was good. Gimmicks like domes were good. Steam was *old*.

Stalwarts like N&W held out as long as they could, but the economic tide had shifted. The indispensible place of steam in the evolution of streamlining America—not just America's railroads—was relegated to the history books.

C&O M-1 steam-turbine-electric No. 500 at the Baldwin plant in late 1947, after minor front-end cosmetic modifications to numberboards and handrails. Within the sleek carbody were a coal bunker (in nose), a conventional firebox and boiler (behind cab), and a turbine-generator assembly (in sloping rear portion). Tender carried water only. Electrical current powered diesel-type traction motors on the two four-axle trucks. C&O PHOTO; C&OHS COLLECTION

Nashville, Chattanooga & St. Louis' homebuilt *City of Memphis* of 1947 was America's last stem-to-stern "steamliner." NC&STL PHOTO; TLC COLLECTION

5 NORTHERN PARALLELS

Canadian Pacific 4-4-4 Jubilee No. 2925 led the three cars of train No. 602 through Toronto's Don Valley on June 11, 1956. H. B. Bowen's flat-faced semi-streamlining lent a family appearance to several disparate classes of CPR steam power. AL PATERSON COLLECTION

Events of the 1930s, both economic and esthetic, were mirrored north of the U.S.–Canadian border.

Canada's railroad network was—and remains—inexorably linked with that in the United States. The political border, for the railroads, was long little more than a formality, with railroads from each country sending tendrils into the other. Ranging from remote mountain railheads and Prairie branch lines to the trio of trunk lines that, until the 1980s, operated across Southern Ontario, U.S. railroads have had a long presence on Canadian soil. For their part, Canada's two largest companies exercised corporate control over important links in the American Midwest and Northeast.

It is hardly surprising, then, that both Canadian National and Canadian Pacific were bitten early, and bitten hard, by the streamlining bug. Both railroads were headquartered in eastern Canada—in Montreal—and thus had ringside seats for the show put on by New York Central and Baltimore & Ohio, among others, in the mid-1930s. More than mere observers, however, the Canadians had already put in motion the substantial engineering, research, and design resources at their disposal.

NORTHERN NORTHERNS

During June and July 1936, Canadian National Railways (CNR) took delivery of five Class U-4a 4-8-4s from Montreal Locomotive Works (MLW). Described by the railway as "partially streamlined," the quintet was intended for heavy passenger service on the CNR's busy trunk route between Montreal, Toronto, and the international border at Sarnia (Ont.).

The CNR ultimately owned 203 Northerns—more than any other railroad—along with 83 Mountains (4-8-2). This affinity for eight-coupled engines stemmed, largely, from the status of the Canadian National as a post-First World War amalgam of a number of failing or undermaintained railroads. Eight drivers spread a locomotive's weight enough that the seemingly endless miles of less-than-perfect trackage could be navigated with a minimum of peril. Competitor Canadian Pacific, on the other hand, with its comparatively better infrastructure, embraced the 4-6-4 as its latter-day heavy passenger wheel arrangement of choice.

Design work on the streamlining for Canadian National's U-4 locomotives had begun in 1931—well before the *Commodore Vanderbilt's* widely publicized debut—as a series of wind tunnel tests conducted on models at the National Research Council (NRC) in Ottawa (Ont.). The Assistant Director of the NRC's Department of Physics, J. H. Parkin, assigned the task to physicist and aerodynamicist John J. Green.

Using a pair of 1:12 scale models (one inch to the foot) of the CNR's most recent 6100-series Northerns—one made of steel and the other of wood—Green developed several potential shroud configurations in conjunction with CNR motive power officials. The railway, and the government, had imposed a number of restrictions on the NRC's streamlining freedom, ranging from the placement of safety appliances and a desire to keep running gear uncovered to the goal of achieving the greatest aerodynamic benefit with the minimum possible cost and complexity.

The objective was more practical than esthetic: to reduce or eliminate the tendency of smoke to obscure vision from the cab while the locomotive was "drifting," when low speed and ambient air currents could combine to blow exhaust smoke down over the boiler and across the cab.

In a progression of modifications to the wind tunnel models, Green added a hemispherical nose, then a skyline casing, then altered the skyline and the angle of the cab front, and added a teardrop fairing around the stack. The next major change was the downward extension of the smokebox cover to merge with a smoothed pilot, all the while with Green computing improved resistance and observing air flow over the engine at various speeds. The final U-4a design was emerging, along with a decision to leave the Vanderbilt tenders unshrouded—the object of the exercise being, after all, the improvement of air flow over the boiler and cab.

The CNR acted on Green's data, which had received trade exposure in a May 1933 *Railway Age* article, by placing two orders for a total of eleven streamlined Northerns. Five were built by MLW in 1936 as Class U-4a (Nos. 6400-6404), and six nearly identical twins were built by Lima in 1938 for U.S. subsidiary Grand Trunk Western. GTW Nos. 6405-6410 were classed as U-4b, and differed from their elder cousins most obviously in the design of the skyline casings' grilled forward end. The CNR engines' convex, horizontally grilled opening contrasted with a concave, vertically slotted arrangement on the GTW engines.

The CNR promoted the newly arrived U-4a's as "indicative of the progress made by the Canadian National Railways" during the 100 years since July 21, 1836—the first run of the locomotive *Dorchester* on Canada's first railway, the 16-mile Champlain & St. Lawrence in Quebec. During "a century of service," the C&StL had become part of the CNR system, and railway publicists of 1936 thrilled readers with comparisons between the two locomotives. The 330-ton, 95-foot-long No.

Smoke control may have been the main reason for their streamlining, but Canadian National got plenty of promotional mileage from the U-4a's modern looks in 1930s publicity materials like these.
AUTHOR'S COLLECTION

CNR U-4a No. 6402 was being serviced at Windsor, Ontario, in 1940. Marker lights and whistle location did little for the engines' streamlining, although the bell was tucked away behind the skyline casing grill. DAVE SHAW COLLECTION

No. 6404 was about 21 miles from its destination as it led Toronto-bound train No. 94, the *Maple Leaf*, through Oakville, Ontario, on its overnight journey from Philadelphia and New York City on March 22, 1958. The train was operated in conjunction with the Lehigh Valley Railroad, and included an LV combine (the second car visible) and through Philadelphia–Toronto and New York–Toronto heavyweight Pullmans in its consist. AL PATERSON COLLECTION

The U-4b's purchased in 1938 for CNR subsidiary Grand Trunk Western differed slightly from their older Canadian cousins, most noticeably in the design of their skyline casing air intakes. The grillwork and upper nose of the GTW engines were painted silver. No. 6410 led the *Inter-City Limited* through South Bend, Ind., in May 1946. WILLIAM A. RAIA COLLECTION

Grand Trunk Western passenger trains used Dearborn Station as their Chicago terminal. GTW U-4b No. 6408 treads through the multiple diamonds of the 21st Street interlocking, a short distance south of the station, with the Montreal-bound *International Limited* on June 15, 1953. The CNR acquired its first lightweight passenger cars in the late 1930s and modernized scores of heavyweights after the war, making trains pulled by the U-4s an eclectic mixture of car designs. DAVE SHAW COLLECTION

6400 was contrasted with "its remote parent," the 16-ton *Dorchester* and its 85-foot train: "Thus, this mammoth of the steel highway was in itself longer than the entire pioneer train of 100 years ago."

The U-4a's weighed 236,000 pounds on their 77-inch drivers, with a total engine weight of 379,800 pounds. Boiler pressure was 275 PSI, cylinders measured 24x30, and 52,000 pounds of tractive force was exerted. Tenders held 11,700 Imperial gallons of water and 20 tons of coal, and rode on six-wheel trucks.

The well-insulated vestibule-type cabs were equipped with a spinning-disk front window on the engineer's side. The centrifugal force of the rotating glass threw off rain and snow to maintain clear vision. A curved gusset filled the joint between front cab wall and running board, and was one of the measures specified by Green to improve air flow.

The green paint of the tender and cab continued forward along the wide running board skirting, edged in gold, before tapering to a shallow "V" on the lower nose. The nose itself was black, as was the portion of the skyline casing and jacket corresponding to the smokebox. The balance of the boiler jacket was planished steel, and the running gear was black. Identification was provided by a pair of illuminated numberboards partially recessed into the upper nose, and the CNR's trademark red-filled brass number plate below the headlight. Cast brass numerals were applied to the running board skirts, and a CANADIAN NATIONAL monogram (GRAND TRUNK WESTERN on the U-4b's) appeared on the flat sides of the tender coal bunker.

As striking as they were, the CNR system's only truly streamlined steam locomotives were deemed unworthy of duplication. Bullet noses, flanged stacks, and striped running board skirts—but no other attempts at streamlined styling—placed CNR Class U-1f 4-8-2s Nos. 6060-6079 firmly in the "bandwagon" league with the likes of the NC&StL's 4-8-4 Dixies, as did the green paint and running board skirts applied by CNR to K-5a Hudsons 5700-5704 of 1930. The U-1f's were built by MLW in late 1944, and proved to be the final new steam locomotives acquired by Canadian National. Prior to retirement (which was as late as April 1960 for some), the "Bullet Nose Bettys," as they were nicknamed, lost their only real claim to fame—their conical noses were removed at Winnipeg in favor of a more conventional smokebox door arrangement.

GTW U-4b No. 6405 lasted in revenue service until autumn 1959—as did Norfolk & Western Class J No. 611—to bring down the curtain on streamlined steam in the United States. The U-4b was not as lucky as its N&W counterpart, however, as all of the GTW streamliners were scrapped.

"Streamlined" only by dint of their conical noses, Canadian National's 19 Class U-1f 4-8-2s were built by MLW in 1944 and were the CNR's last new steam power. "Bullet Nose Betty" No. 6068 left Brantford, Ont., under a Vesuvian cloud in July 1958.
HAROLD K. VOLLRATH COLLECTION

THE ROYAL TREATMENT

History was made in the spring of 1939 when a reigning British monarch set foot on North American soil for the first time. With war clouds looming over Europe, the visit of King George VI and Queen Elizabeth was seen as a means of encouraging, and cementing, solidarity in the face of the approaching crisis—as events unfolded, Britain and Canada were both at war with Germany barely two months after the King and Queen had returned to England.

The Canadian government, led by Prime Minister William Lyon Mackenzie King, was determined to put on the country's best face for the royal visitors, and entrusted Canada's two transcontinental

Resplendent in its special blue livery, CNR U-4a No. 6400 waited to assume its Royal Train duties at Ottawa, Ont., on May 21, 1939. A total of nine CNR locomotives shared the honors over the course of the Royal Train's 4,212 Canadian National miles.
DAVE SHAW COLLECTION

Canadian Pacific H-1d Hudson No. 2850 pulled the 1939 Royal Train throughout its time on CPR rails, and was photographed near Beavermouth, British Columbia, on May 28. The engine received a stainless steel boiler jacket for the occasion, along with a blue and aluminum livery in place of its regular maroon. Royal coats of arms were mounted on the tender and upper nose, and a crown adorned the forward edge of each running board. So successful was No. 2850 in its Royal Train duties that the engine's designer, H. B. Bowen, sought and received permission to affix cast crowns to all 45 of the CPR's semi-streamlined 4-6-4s—known thereafter as Royal Hudsons.
CPR PHOTO; AUTHOR'S COLLECTION

railways with the task of transporting the royal entourage and associated members of the press from East to West and back. Every one of the country's nine provinces was visited (Newfoundland did not join Confederation until 1949), as were the federal and provincial capitals and major population and industrial centers.

Assembled by the CNR, CPR, and Canadian government, the 12-car Royal Train conveyed and accommodated King George VI and Queen Elizabeth on their precedent-setting 30-day tour (including a four-day side trip to the United States encompassing Washington, DC, and the New York World's Fair). The train consisted of four CNR and six CPR cars, along with two cars owned by the Canadian government for the use of the Governor General (the monarch's Canadian representative). For their special duty, the 12 cars were given a royal blue livery, with gold-outlined window bands of aluminum leaf and gun-metal roofs.

Both the CNR and CPR assigned steam locomotives to lead the Royal Train and its accompanying 12-car pilot train over their respective lines.

U-4a No. 6400 was selected to lead the Royal Train over some of its eastern CNR mileage. A total of nine other CNR locomotives—none streamlined—also led the Royal Train in the course of its journey. Unlike Canadian Pacific, which employed H-1d Hudson No. 2850 throughout, the CNR assigned engines from the territory through which the Royal Train would pass. Streamlined No. 6400 pulled the train from Ottawa to Toronto on May 21, and from Toronto to Niagara Falls (via London, Ont.) on June 7. Sister No. 6401 was assigned to the pilot train for the same June 7 itinerary. The CNR engines—and CPR counterpart No. 2850—were also given predominantly blue paint schemes adorned by royal coats of arms, running board crowns, and a gold-edged aluminum band on the after portion of their tenders corresponding with the trailing cars' window band.

The pilot train accommodated the press and others not directly connected with the royal party, and normally preceded the Royal Train by 30 minutes. On one occasion, en route to Washington Union Station to meet President and Mrs. Roosevelt on June 8, the pilot train developed an overheated journal near Montgomery, Pa., and was passed by the Royal Train—reporters and photographers on the stricken train missed the ceremonies in Union Station's Presidential waiting room.

From May 18, the day after their arrival at Quebec City aboard the Canadian Pacific liner *Empress of Australia*, until their June 15 departure from Halifax aboard the *Empress of Britain*, the King and Queen traveled 9,150 miles by rail. (A short portion of that was behind another notable streamlined steam locomotive—one of New York Central's Dreyfuss-styled J-3a Hudsons led the Royal Train north from New York City on June 11 en route back to eastern Canada.)

Following their active Royal Train duty, CNR No. 6400 and CPR No. 2850 were dispatched to the New York World's Fair for display and performing roles in the "Railroads on Parade" pageant. Fittingly, they debuted on Dominion Day, July 1, Canada's national holiday. No. 6400 traveled to the Fair under its own steam over CNR subsidiary Central Vermont as far as Springfield, Mass., south of which weight and clearance restrictions required the tender to be emptied and the engine hauled dead to Flushing Meadows. Upon their return to Canada, both engines resumed regular service and, fittingly, both were preserved as museum pieces.

BOWEN'S BEAUTIES

Henry Blane Bowen had 23 years of Canadian Pacific Railway service under his belt when he was appointed the CPR's Chief of Motive Power and Rolling Stock in 1928.

Bowen, an Englishman by birth, created a body of work from the mid-1930s through 1949 that flavored the CPR's passenger trains with vaguely British undertones and a dash of Midwestern spice.

In 1936, the CPR unveiled a quartet of streamlined, lightweight four-car trains along with five streamlined Class F-2a 4-4-4 steam locomotives to pull them.

Each four-car train comprised a mail-express car, a baggage-buffet-coach, and two full coaches. Initially, two consists were assigned to 173-mile Montreal–Quebec City runs, one entered service over the 229 miles between Toronto and Detroit as the *Royal York*, and the fourth consist became the 194-mile Calgary–Edmonton (Alta.) *Chinook*. The Toronto–Detroit and Quebec City–Montreal rotations each were assigned two of the new 4-4-4s, with the fifth engine looking after the Alberta schedule on its own.

Cast in the *Hiawatha* mold, the new CPR trains departed from Milwaukee Road's year-old precedent in the manner of their engines' smokebox streamlining and the number and configuration of cars.

The smooth, welded sides of the CPR cars curved slightly inward at the top and bottom, with sides and roof merging almost seamlessly. Sides were painted in the CPR's traditional maroon, with roof and underbody black. Square-cornered,

With a trio of homebuilt lightweight cars in tow, Canadian Pacific F-2a Jubilee No. 3000 sprints through Cooksville, Ontario, on February 5, 1949, as Toronto–Detroit train No. 629. Cosmetic changes over the 13 years since the engine's delivery include removal of the streamlined stack fairing and placement of a larger illuminated numberboard in the upper nose where the smoke deflector air intake used to be. The original retractable coupler has also given way to a fixed version, but with minimum disruption to the engine's deep pilot shroud.
AL PATERSON COLLECTION

CPR F-1a Jubilee No. 2914 was a 1938 product of the Canadian Locomotive Company. The 4-4-4 was photographed at Brandon, Manitoba, in October 1952. Note the extension above the original streamlined stack fairing. HAROLD K. VOLLRATH COLLECTION

Jubilee No. 2928 was leading train No. 637 from Hamilton to Guelph Junction, Ont., and a connection to Goderich on the shore of Lake Huron. The train climbed the Niagara Escarpment at Waterdown, Ont., in 1955. This was one of two CPR Jubilees to be preserved; the other was No. 2929. AL PATERSON COLLECTION

vertically oriented windows evoked the 1935 *Hiawatha*, and the broader parallel was more than coincidental. Karl Nystrom—responsible for much of the *Hiawathas'* engineering and design as superintendent of the Milwaukee Road's car department at the time—had worked as a colleague of Bowen's in the capacity of the CPR Car Department's Chief Draftsman between 1918 and 1920. During that period, Bowen had been the CPR Mechanical Department's Chief Draftsman, based in Winnipeg but in close contact with the railway's Montreal headquarters.

The car frames were built in Hamilton, Ontario, by National Steel Car, with the balance of construction taking place at the CPR's Angus shops in Montreal.

The basic architecture and construction methods of the new CPR lightweight cars would persist through 1949, when wide-windowed 2200-series coaches and a group of 19 *Grove*-series 10 roomette-5 bedroom sleepers (near clones of Pullman-Standard's *Cascade*-series floor plan) brought CPR in-house passenger car construction to a close.

Similarly, the smooth styling created for the 3000-series F-2a Jubilees of 1936 was reprised in slightly modified form on three more groups of CPR steam locomotives introduced during Bowen's tenure as Chief of "MP&RS."

As for the CPR F-2a 4-4-4s—built by Alco affiliate Montreal Locomotive Works (MLW)—their wraparound pilot design, cylinder skirting, and boiler jacket all emulated the Milwaukee Road Class A Atlantics of 1935. Bowen gave his Jubilees a broad, smooth smokebox front, barely convex in cross section. A flush-mounted headlight was centered on the nose, and, as built, a grilled air intake occupied the upper fifth of the circle. The only protrusion atop the boiler jacket was a stack fairing, teardrop-shaped in plan—harking back to one element of John Green's published NRC research leading up to the CNR U-4 design—with an integral illuminated numberboard on either side. A pair of teardrop marker light housings was mounted at the point where the chrome handrails curved onto and down over the nose in a deep "U" shape. Vestibule-type cabs had become common in Canada, given the difficult winters, and Bowen integrated two-foot-deep running board skirts into the Jubilees' cab sides. No attempt was made to streamline the forward half of the tender, with its angular coal bunker, but the aft portion matched the height and approximate cross-section of the new lightweight cars.

Tenders rode on four-wheel trucks and could carry 12 tons of coal and 7,000 Imperial gallons of water.

F-2a's Nos. 3000-3004 placed 120,000 pounds (of a total 263,000) on their 80-inch drivers, and operated with a boiler pressure of 300 PSI. Cylinders measured 17.25x28 inches. Tractive force was a modest 26,500 pounds, but was deemed ample for the short, fast trains the 4-4-4s were designed to pull.

And speedsters they were. No. 3003 established the highest officially recorded speed for a steam locomotive in Canada with a September 18, 1936, sprint to 112.5 MPH outside St. Telesphore, Quebec.

Gloss black paint was relieved by planished steel on the boiler jacket aft of the smokebox, and gold-edged maroon panels on the running board skirts, cab sides, and tender. A pair of polished metal bands wrapped around the smooth pilot, behind which was concealed a retractable coupler. Lettering was gold, and a multi-colored CPR crest adorned each side of the cab.

The retractable couplers were dispensed with after a few years, and by the late 1940s the grill in the upper nose had been replaced with a single large illuminated numberboard in lieu of the originals flanking the stack. The bell migrated atop the boiler jacket from its original position beneath the left-side front cowling, where it was somewhat muffled and prone to snow and ice clogging.

Next in the CPR's streamlined stable were 20 lightweight 2900-series Class F-1a 4-4-4s built by CLC in 1937–38. Nos. 2910-2929 were more diminutive counterparts to the F-2a's, with 75-inch drivers, 16.5x28 cylinders, 26,000 pounds of tractive force, and 240,000 pounds engine weight. Boiler pressure, however, remained at 300 PSI.

Bowen abandoned the wraparound pilot and clean-topped boiler jacket with these, and subsequent, streamlined engines. A smooth prow pilot was surmounted by an angled, flat sheet leading up to the underside of the smokebox. The running board skirting continued forward and down at an angle to meet the pilot beam. This improved access to the cylinders and other front-end equipment, which was one of the main reasons Bowen had opted for what he termed a "semi-streamlined" form in the first place.

The best-known of Canadian Pacific's steam locomotives—to students of railroad history and the general public alike—were the final 45 Hudsons of the 65-engine-strong 2800-series. All built by MLW, the semi-streamlined engines comprised three subclasses and arrived in three groups between 1937 and 1948.

Nos. 2820-2849 arrived as Class H-1c in 1937; Nos. 2850-2859 were built as Class H-1d in mid-1938; and oil-burning H-1e Nos. 2860-2864 were delivered for western service in June 1940. Streamlining on these 45 Hudsons mirrored that applied to the F-1a Jubilees.

Bowen's strong "family" appearance was upheld with these semi-streamlined Hudsons. Their clean, cylindrical boiler jackets were blemished only by a turbogenerator and safety valve turret (and, later, the bell) ahead of the cab, and barely perceptible blisters beside the forward portion of the stack fairing covering the

ends of the Elesco feedwater heater. Like the earlier Jubilees, these Hudsons' cabs were given radiused front corners.

The oil-burning H-1e's, assigned to mainline passenger duties in British Columbia, were delivered with a smaller stack fairing and an enlarged and relocated numberboard arrangement that would be retrofitted to the H-1c's and H-1d's. A single illuminated number glass was placed in the upper portion of the "full moon" smokebox front, greatly improving identification from the front.

The Hudsons rode on 75-inch drivers, had a boiler pressure of 275 PSI, employed 22x30-inch cylinders, weighed 186,800 pounds on drivers against a total engine weight of 354,000 pounds, and exerted 45,250 pounds of tractive force. Fifteen of the engines—H-1c's Nos. 2838-2842, H-1d's Nos. 2850-2854, and H-1e's 2860-2864—were equipped with boosters

Booster-equipped H-1c Royal Hudson No. 2838 had a mix of heavyweight Toronto, Hamilton & Buffalo Railway and lightweight New York Central cars on its drawbar as it led Toronto-bound train No. 712 through Oakville, Ont., on June 15, 1957. This train, running here on CNR trackage rights, was one of several joint CPR-TH&B-NYC schedules linking Toronto via through sleeping cars with points across the U.S. Northeast. AL PATERSON COLLECTION

H-1d Royal Hudson No. 2857 led Detroit-bound train No. 629 through Chatham, Ont., on August 21, 1947. All five cars were built on purchased frames at the CPR's Angus shops. DAVE SHAW COLLECTION

No. 2860 was an oil-burning H-1e assigned to British Columbia, and one of the final group of Royal Hudsons built, in 1940. With the H-1e's came an abbreviated stack fairing, and an enlarged and relocated number indicator. Photographed at Vancouver in May 1955, this locomotive would earn celebrity as an excursion leader beginning in the 1970s. AL PATERSON COLLECTION

CPR T-1b Selkirk No. 5928 led train No. 4, the transcontinental *Dominion*, east into the Connaught Tunnel at Glacier, B.C., on August 31, 1940. The hulking 2-10-4s, with their distinctive beveled cab sides, were originally employed on freight and passenger trains between Calgary (Alta.) and Revelstoke (B.C.), and later ran east of Calgary to Swift Current (Sask.). AL PATERSON COLLECTION

adding another 12,000 pounds of tractive force. The booster-equipped engines—weighing 363,100 pounds in total with 186,700 on drivers—were selectively assigned to runs in northern Ontario and the West having heavy grades.

Tenders rode on a pair of six-wheel trucks and held 12,000 Imperial gallons of water and either 21 tons of coal or, on the H-1e's, 4,100 Imperial gallons of fuel oil.

The CPR's sleek Hudsons gained their collective fame through the celebrity of No. 2850, selected to pull the 1939 Royal Train over the Canadian Pacific portion of its route. So exemplary was the performance of No. 2850 and pilot train locomotive No. 2851 during more than 3,200 miles of closely scrutinized duties that Bowen sought, and received, royal permission to place cast crowns—like the ones that had graced No. 2850 during the tour—on the forward running board

skirts of all 45 streamlined 4-6-4s. As a result, CPR classes H-1c, H-1d, and H-1e were known thereafter as Royal Hudsons.

No. 2850 followed up its stint on the Royal Train with an appearance—along with its regal associate, CNR No. 6400—at the 1939 New York World's Fair. The blue-and-stainless steel Hudson made its way from Toronto to New York via CPR subsidiary Toronto, Hamilton & Buffalo, then over Michigan Central, New York Central, West Shore, and Boston & Albany to Chatham, N.Y. From that point the engine proceeded down NYC's Harlem Division to the New Haven Railroad, across Hell Gate Bridge to a Long Island Railroad connection, and on to the Fairgrounds.

Although they saw service across Canada, the Royal Hudsons were long assigned in clusters to various regions. Nos. 2820-2828 and 2858-2859 were Montreal-based; Nos. 2829-2837 and 2843-2849 were assigned to service in the Prairie provinces and based in Winnipeg; booster-equipped Nos. 2838-2842 held down assignments on the *Dominion* and other heavy transcontinental schedules between Toronto and Fort William (Ont.) via the north shore of Lake Superior; Nos. 2850-2854 ran on the same trains between Fort William and Winnipeg; Nos. 2855-2857 were based in Toronto; and Nos. 2860-2864 called Revelstoke (B.C.) and Vancouver home.

In British Columbia, the Royal Hudsons were augmented by semi-streamlined 2-10-4 Selkirks. These arrived from MLW in two groups: Nos. 5920-5929 (Class T-1b) in 1939 and Nos. 5930-5935 (Class T-1c)—reflecting Bowen's optimism in the future

of the steam locomotive—in 1949. Both Selkirk classes shared 63-inch drivers, 25x32-inch cylinders, 285 PSI boiler pressure, and 88,900 pounds of boosted tractive force. The T-1b's had a total engine weight of 447,000 pounds, while the T-1c's were a ton heavier. Weight on drivers was 309,900 pounds. The Selkirks saw service on the *Dominion* and other CPR transcontinental trains, and were also regularly employed in mountain freight service. In the words of the builder, "the design is the CPR standard 2-10-4 type, modernized and streamlined to conform with their modern 4-4-4 type and 4-6-4 type, thereby continuing the same pleasing, striking appearance for all their new power built for mainline service."

Appearance notwithstanding, the influx of GM FP7s and other boiler-equipped diesel models after 1952 marked the beginning of the end for steam locomotives on CPR passenger trains across the country. The last revenue run for one of Bowen's semi-streamlined engines occurred in Montreal commuter service in 1960. Four Royal Hudsons, including celebrity No. 2850, survived scrapping. Two of these, Nos. 2839 and 2860, went on to excursion careers of varying scope.

CASING COUSIN

With important Canadian National connections at North Bay and Cochrane, Ontario, and Rouyn, Quebec, the Temiskaming & Northern Ontario Railway (T&NO) was dependent upon the CNR for most of its interchange business. (The T&NO changed its name to the Ontario Northland Railway in April 1946, to avoid the administrative confusion of sharing initials with the Texas & New Orleans.) T&NO passenger trains reached the major offline terminal of Toronto over CNR rails south of North Bay. Both roads shared the status of government wards—the CNR a federal entity and T&NO under Ontario provincial authority—and the T&NO's motive power reflected elements of Canadian National influence.

Nowhere was this more apparent than in the streamlining of T&NO 4-6-2 No. 700, the 1940 recipient of a nose cowling, skyline casing, running boards, and cab clearly inspired by the CNR's U-4a design. Built by the Canadian Locomotive Company (CLC) in 1921 as the first of four

69-inch-drivered Pacifics originally numbered 157-160, No. 700's 1940 rebuilding also included valve gear and tender modifications. The cowling's smoke-lifting abilities appear to have been limited since, within a couple of years, large "elephant ear" smoke deflectors were added to No. 700's front end. Sister No. 701 and and a quartet of CLC 4-8-4s (Nos. 1100-1103) built in 1936–37 received similar running board, smoke deflector, and cab modifications after 1942. No. 700 eventually lost its shrouded nose and skyline casing.

Over the years, No. 700 and its unstreamlined roster mates accented their basic black paint with different combinations of red or green running board striping and tender name panels, with Ontario's provincial coat of arms adorning cab sides and smoke deflectors. Tender lettering read ONTARIO NORTHLAND after the 1946 name change.

An influx of General Motors FP7A's after 1951 bumped Ontario Northland's Pacifics and Northerns from their established runs, the most important of which was the overnight Toronto–Timmins (Ont.) *Northland*.

Pacific No. 700 was scrapped in 1957, two years after No. 703 met a similar fate. No. 701 had the bittersweet honor of leading the ONR's symbolic final steam trip in June 1957, and was preserved (as was No. 702, which had been sold to the Quebec, North Shore & Labrador in 1953). The ONR's four Northerns were scrapped.

Even with the addition of elephant ear smoke deflectors, there was an unmistakable lineage of CNR U-4a in Temiskaming & Northern Ontario's Pacific No. 700, at North Bay, Ontario, on September 12, 1943. DAVE SHAW COLLECTION

6 THE SPECTRUM

LEFT: Reading's stainless steel *Crusader*.
© MICHAEL F. KOTOWSKI; REPRODUCED WITH PERMISSION

TOP: Southern Railway Ps-4 Pacific No. 1380 was Otto Kuhler's favorite—and final—streamlined steam commission. BOB'S PHOTOS

ABOVE: Chesapeake & Ohio L-1 Hudson No. 492 was one of four rebuilt and modernized Pacifics shrouded to handle connecting schedules of the *Chessie*. C&OHS COLLECTION

OVERLEAF: "Pennsylvaniasaurus." A T-1 under wire at Harrisburg, Pennsylvania. © TED ROSE; REPRODUCED WITH PERMISSION

"Thanks, Pop." A hometown
crowd on the Milwaukee Road.
© TED ROSE; REPRODUCED
WITH PERMISSION

153

The Texas & New Orleans'
Sunbeam. © MICHAEL F. KOTOWSKI;
REPRODUCED WITH PERMISSION

The St. Louis-San Francisco's
Firefly. © MICHAEL F. KOTOWSKI;
REPRODUCED WITH PERMISSION

ENDNOTES

CHAPTER 1

1 Haslam, Malcolm, *In the Deco Style*, p. 158

2 Hillier, Bevis, *The Style of the Century*, p. 97

3 United States Department of Commerce, "Report of the Commission on the 1925 Paris Exposition,' Washington, DC, 1926

4 Escritt, Stephen; Bevis Hillier, *Art Deco Style*, p. 87

5 Ibid, p. 84

6 *Railway Age*, October 14, 1939, p. 554

BIBLIOGRAPHY

BOOKS

Archer, Eric [Ed.], *Streamlined Steam*, Quadrant Press, New York, 1972

Car Builders' Cyclopedia 1949–1951, Simmons-Boardman Publishing, New York

Castner, Charles; Robert Chapman; Patrick Dorin, *Louisville & Nashville Passenger Trains—The Pan American Era*, TLC Publishing, Lynchburg, Va., 1999

Cook, Richard J., *New York Central's Mercury*, TLC Publishing, Lynchburg, Va., 1991

Escritt, Stephen; Bevis Hillier, *Art Deco Style*, Phaidon Press, London, 1997

Goolsby, Larry, *Atlanta Birmingham & Coast*, ACL/SAL Historical Society, Valrico, Fla., 2000.

Greenberg, William; Frederick Kramer, *The Handsomest Trains in the World*, Quadrant Press, New York, 1978

Haslam, Malcolm; Dan Klein; Nancy McClelland, *In the Deco Style*, Rizzoli, New York, 1986

Hillier, Bevis, *The Style of the Century*, E. P. Dutton, New York, 1986

Loewy, Raymond, *Industrial Design*, Overlook Press, Woodstock, N.Y., 1979

Miller, Ken, *Norfolk & Western Passenger Service 1946–1971*, TLC Publishing, Lynchburg, Va., 2000

Randall, David, *From Zephyr to Amtrak*, Prototype Publications, Park Forest, Ill., 1972

Ransome-Wallis, P., *The Last Steam Locomotives of British Railways*, 3rd Edition, Magna Books, Leicester, England, 1993

Scribbins, Jim, *The Hiawatha Story*, Kalmbach Publishing Company, Milwaukee, Wis., 1970

Welsh, Joe, *Pennsy Streamliners—The Blue Ribbon Fleet*, Kalmbach Publishing Company, Waukesha, Wis., 1999

Who's Who in Railroading, 12th Edition, Simmons-Boardman Publishing, New York, 1949

PERIODICALS

Allen, Cecil, "126 Miles Per Hour—With Steam!," *Trains*, Kalmbach Publishing Co., September 1956

Anderson, Willard, "The Century-old C&EI," *Trains*, Kalmbach Publishing Co., August 1949

Baldwin Locomotives, Baldwin Locomotive Works, October 1936; April 1937; October 1937; October 1939; October 1940; December 1942; Second Quarter 1945

Brown, James and Omer Lavalee, "Hudson Royalty," *Trains*, Kalmbach Publishing Co., August 1969

Dunn, Ralph, "The Presidents, B&O's Super Pacifics," *Trains*, Kalmbach Publishing Co., June 1951

Canada 1940, Dominion Bureau of Statistics, Department of Trade & Commerce, Ottawa, 1940

Emmott, N. W., "How to Streamline a Steam Locomotive," *Trains*, Kalmbach Publishing Co., March 1973

Kalmbach, A.C., "Epoch of Electrification," *Trains*, Kalmbach Publishing Co., April 1946

Lanctot, Gustave, "The King and Queen Visit Their Kingdom of Canada," *Canadian Geographical Journal*, Vol. XIX No. 1, July 1939

Morgan, David, "Otto Kuhler, an Original," *Trains*, Kalmbach Publishing Co., October 1975

Pond, C.E., "4-8-0's to Mallets to Jawn Henry," *Trains*, Kalmbach Publishing Co., October 1984

Railway Age, Simmons-Boardman Publishing Co., various 1933–1956

Reed, Brian, "The American 4-8-4," *Loco Profile 20*, Profile Publications, January 1972

Rung, Al, "He Styles the Streamliners," *Trains*, Kalmbach Publishing Co., December 1948

Stagner, Lloyd, "Blue Goose and Kin," *Trains*, Kalmbach Publishing Co., June 1985

Tillotson, Curt, "The Rest of the Story," *Ties*, Southern Rwy Historical Association, May-June 2002